WATCHERS
in the
MORNING

A spirituality for contemporary Christians

Graeme
Rutherford

D1743366

Foreword by George Carey

CollinsDove
An imprint of HarperCollins*Publishers*

To Caroline

whose unquestioning faith is marked by monastic simplicity,
whose enthusiastic welcome to visitors outstrips monastic hospitality,
whose ready laughter is the perfect foil to my need for monastic silence.

A Collins Dove publication
An imprint of HarperCollins*Melbourne*
22–24 Joseph Street
North Blackburn, Victoria 3130, Australia

First published 1994
Designed by John van Loon
Cover design by John van Loon
Cover photograph by Helga Leunig
Photography by Helga Leunig
Typeset in Australia by HarperCollins*Melbourne*
Printed in Australia by McPherson's Printing Group

The National Library of Australia
Cataloguing-in-Publication Data:

Rutherford, Graeme S.
  Watchers in the morning.
  ISBN 1 86371 404 9.
  1. Spirituality. 2. Spiritual life — Christianity.
  3. Christian life — 1960– . I. Title.

FOREWORD

I had no difficulty accepting Graeme Rutherford's kind invitation to write this foreword. Not only is he a good friend but he is also a dear colleague who served with me in St Nicholas' Durham and went through the 'waters of change' with us all. Knowing the measure of the man, I knew that whatever he wrote would repay serious study.

But when I started to read the manuscript I discovered another reason for complying with his request. Quite simply this book is an important contribution to the Decade of Evangelism and the life of the Church. For too long we have separated the active work of Church growth from the contemplative life of prayer. Frequently, many Christians have seen their task as getting on with the job of promoting the faith with only a brief cheerful nod of acknowledgement for the monastic way.

'Yes,' they have conceded, 'the work of monasteries is important — for those who like that sort of thing. But for us — no thank you very much.'

Graeme shares his story with us; a story rooted in Anglican evangelicalism and one which continues to be deeply grateful to that tradition's firm commitment to scripture, personal holiness and the Lordship of Christ. When he attended Tarrawarra Abbey he was disturbed to see how wrong were the impressions he had formed over the years about monasticism, and how much he had to re-learn. He began to see how the spirituality of monasticism related to life and to every kind of human community. His book shows that Benedictine spirituality is not of a special kind, for 'souped-up' holy people only, but is a way of walking with God that is open to all. He began to scrutinise his own life from this perspective and to see how 'work related' and 'activity-driven' his own spirituality was.

But his life of prayer was not the only thing changed by the experience of Tarrawarra. Graeme's book leads us into consideration of the Bible and the Holy Communion where, for him, richer dimensions of spirituality emerged with transforming results. Again, it is the holistic approach to the Bible and the sacraments that Graeme Rutherford promotes. On the Bible he writes that it should be: 'read in a way that involves the whole person'. On the Holy Communion he writes that: 'The grace given in the Eucharist is not some kind of heavenly substance or medicine. Rather it is Christ himself as spiritual food who takes possession of us and transforms us'.

Our guide to the treasures of Benedictine spirituality will not allow us to view them as an esoteric religiosity for the elite or a prop for the spiritually enervated — Graeme's conviction is that here are treasures to be shared with all.

I have long been convinced of Graeme Rutherford's abilities as a scholar, but I am now convinced of his ability to make rich theological and spiritual ideas accessible to us all. Here is a deceptively simple book that manages to combine complex thoughts, winsome quotations and ready Australian humour, in a mix that I am sure will help many people to know God better.

In England, a warning is required on all cigarette packets that reads: 'Government Health Warning. Cigarettes can seriously damage your health'. Perhaps this book should have been marked: 'Church Health Warning. This book can seriously revolutionise your life!' It is my hope and prayer that it will.

George Carey
Archbishop of Canterbury

CONTENTS

PREFACE

Some of the material in this book originated in Retreat addresses prepared for clergy in the Australian Anglican dioceses of Bendigo, Gippsland, Rockhampton and Adelaide. I am grateful to the respective Bishops, some of whom have now retired, for giving me such opportunities for ministry, and for the clergy of those dioceses for the way in which they responded to the material by sharing themselves with me. In every case I received more in return by way of blessing than they can possibly know.

I am especially indebted to those people who read the manuscript from multiple perspectives. I have benefited enormously from their insights and expertise. Among them are the Rev. Dr Charles Sherlock, Dr Muriel Porter and Fr Michael Casey OCSO.

Professor C. E. B. Cranfield's name occurs with some frequency in the early pages of the text and where his name does not, many of his ideas do. It was he who first stimulated my interest in New Testament eschatology and the homilies of John Chrysostom. As an admirer of John Calvin he may well be surprised as to where my continuing studies have led me. I do not really believe that the spiritual resonances beneath our respective theologies are all that different. The one word he uses to describe Calvin's commentaries is the same word I would use to describe Benedict's Rule. It is the word 'humble'.

The Abbot of Tarrawarra Abbey, Dom David Tomlins, generously wrote letters of introduction to the abbots of the Irish mother and grandmother houses of his monastery, where I was received in true Benedictine style during a period of long-service leave in 1991. Words cannot convey the sense of excitement with which I set out from Ballybrophy on the little branch line train to Roscrea. I had heard much from the beloved

Irish monks of Tarrawarra about the home they had left behind forever and I was thrilled to be able to discover something of their family roots.

Monks do not readily come into most people's minds as the subject for a marketable book in the modern world. I record my thanks to Kevin Mark, religious publisher of Collins Dove, for his confidence that there is something here that the modern world badly needs to hear and heed.

Finally, I thank the Archbishop of Canterbury for his willingness to write the foreword. It is just as well I did not know that he was destined to rise to his present eminence when I was his curate. I would never have had the courage to say then some of the things that I did! And I am eternally grateful that as a boss he instinctively imbibed the spirit of Benedict's advice to Abbots not to scrape off the rust too quickly, lest a hole be left in the metal!

MONKS, MAGPIES AND MYSTERY

A UNIQUE AUSTRALIAN COMMUNITY

A building, simple and humble and almost hidden in the hills' is how architect Paul Archibald described the Cistercian Abbey of Tarrawarra in the lush green Yarra Valley some thirty kilometres from Melbourne. It is a description that captures not only the style of architecture but the hidden and humble form of spirituality lived out by the monks who make up this unique Australian community.

Tarrawarra is an Aboriginal word, probably meaning 'white cloak' and referring to the mist that hangs heavily over the river flats, visible from the verandah of the Abbey guest house on any wintry morning. Like the strange cloud that appeared before the Israelites in the desert, this mysterious mass of vapour conveys an eerie sense of what Rudolf Otto called the numinous or 'creature-feeling'.

The Abbey was founded in 1954, when several small groups of monks left their native Ireland and the Abbey of Mount St Joseph, Roscrea, to establish their form of monasticism in Australia. A total of eighteen monks made up the foundation community. Today, with nearly thirty monks, it remains the only Cistercian community in the country.

The original band of Irish monks laboured long and hard on the 405 hectare property to pay off the debt. They acquired modest buildings that had been used as construction workers' huts in the post-war years and turned them into cells for the monks. In due course, the original home on the property became the present guest house. A simple wooden church was built in 1957.

There have been many occasions when I have driven over the cattle grid at the main gate of Tarrawarra and down the dirt track that winds its way up to the tall sugar gums that surround the monastery buildings and felt that I have entered the veritable gate of heaven. The nearby paddocks are dotted with dairy cows and the distinctive white Charolais beef herd grazes peacefully on the distant river flats beneath the old Yarra Glen–Healesville railway-line. In the trees outside the church the magpies warble their exultant paeans of praise. Inside the monks chant psalms:

> I lift up my eyes to the hills — from where will my help come? My help comes from the Lord, who made heaven and earth. (Psalm 121:1,2)

Ora et labora — prayer and work— sums up the life of a monk. Throughout the day he moves from choir to work and work to choir and much of what he comes upon in the psalms is an echo of what he sees in creation. The creation is a primal sacrament of God. The monk's withdrawal to society's fringe is so that he can listen more attentively to God's presence in the created order and society. The 'separation from the world' is not intended to encourage a denial of the created order. The aim is not to escape from the world but to live a more wholesome life within it. God is present in our world and the monastic life forces us to ask ourselves, 'can we see and hear his presence?' It stands as a constant challenge to a generation that, in its desire to remain perpetually youthful, has a fetish for fitness and engages in its daily exercise programme by listening, not to the birds and other natural sounds, but to the radio on headsets. Coming aside from the pressures and tensions of ministry, the Christian worker discovers afresh the reality of what is believed all along. Nothing is learned that is not known but everything is new. The God one teaches and preaches about is the eternal God who is Creator of the hills of the beautiful Yarra Valley and can be enjoyed in the sights, sounds, colours, textures and smells of this hallowed patch of terra firma. But Christian monasticism is not simply a Christian version of the universal phenomenon of monasticism. For the Cistercian Community at Tarrawarra it is a way of following Christ. Being a Christian is primary. It is, fundamentally, watching for the coming of Christ.

MONASTICISM MISUNDERSTOOD

I owe a debt of gratitude to the welcome and acceptance I have received from the Abbot and monks of this community. I do not completely understand how, but my intermittent association with them over a period of nearly twenty years has changed me, not in the way tornadoes change things but in the way that sand is transformed quietly and unobtrusively in an oyster.

Early in my ministry I had heard Dr John Stott, a renowned Anglican Evangelical, stress the importance of study in the life of the Christian minister. I readily approved of his quoting the words of Billy Graham to the effect that 'if he had three more years to live he would spend two in preparation and one in preaching'. A few years later, during a period of ministry in central London, Stott counselled me to pursue further academic theology at Durham University. I will always be grateful for that counsel and the many privileges of that period of study. But an interest in theology is not at all the same thing as knowing God. What the university did not and could not teach me, the monastery, 'simple and humble and almost hidden in the hills', did. Without my being conscious of it, my visits over the years have taught me a new way of praying and reading the Bible. I appreciate more than ever the Benedictine emphasis on the need to lead a balanced life, one that allows both the left and right hemisphere of the brain to be used in a way that my form of cerebral evangelicalism had not. I have learnt to read the Bible with the heart. In the process, I have discovered that there are some things in the Bible that actually seem to subvert the tradition in which I was taught. In my case that was the rather constrained atmosphere of Australian Anglican evangelicalism of the sixties. The Tarrawarra experience has helped me to understand and love the ancient catholic tradition of the Church, and has changed utterly my own spirituality and approach to ministry.

Monasticism was presented to me in my student days as a deeply flawed and profoundly unbiblical movement. It was alleged that the monks misread the biblical message of salvation, either through ignorance, conscious manipulation, or the influence of heterodox thought. That monasticism is unbiblical was especially the complaint of the Reformers and it was through the grid of the Reformers that I was introduced to the subject. No one who knows anything of late medieval monasticism can object to the Reformers' evaluation of the monasticism of that time. It had lost its 'first love'.

No longer was it characterised by the virtues of simplicity and poverty. According to the medieval English reformer, John Wycliffe, monks were 'turned into lords of this world, most idle in God's travail'.

This Reformation critique of monasticism has had a strong influence, especially among Protestant theologians, on the way in which monasticism generally has been perceived and taught. Certainly, those who introduced me to the subject in an Anglican theological college that stands in the Reformed tradition, tended to assume that a movement with such strange practices and ideas could not possibly have sprung from the pure soil of the Gospels. Its origin was sought in neo-Platonism or some other extra-biblical source.

The way in which Protestant theologians handle the monastic image of the ladder is a good example of the way in which early monasticism is misunderstood when interpreted through the Reformation grid. The image is invariably interpreted as running contrary to the gospel of grace. Christian spirituality, we are reminded, is a response spirituality rather than a ladder spirituality. It is too often assumed that the early monastic writers who used the ladder imagery were suggesting a kind of spiritual mountain climbing, as though it were possible by good works and ascetic practices to step up the rungs of the ladder and storm the ramparts of heaven. Undoubtedly the image is open to this kind of misunderstanding and there were those who used it at the time of the Reformation in a way that ran counter to Scripture. But it was never intended to be used as a theological image by Benedict and the early monastics. For them, the image was a guide for behaviour rather than a basis for theology. It was a helpful way of measuring whether or not progress was being made in living out the Christian life.

In chapter seven of his famous sixth-century Rule, Benedict uses the image of 'Jacob's ladder' as a kind of personal vision statement to help his monks see more clearly where they were going. It was intended to help them progress towards humility. Humility, of course, is a virtue that can never be attained by focusing on it. It is our foolish but utterly human tendency to strive to be humble and then find that we have a sneaking regard for the fact that we are getting better at being humble! If we are becoming more humble we should be thinking that we are less humble than we ought to be! As a result of the difficulty involved in this reverse logic many conclude that they can do nothing to rid themselves of their ego-centred drives. They piously imagine that if they are to be humble, God must shower it upon them like manna from heaven. But there is nothing in the Bible that says we are to wait for God to humble us. Instead, we are exhorted to humble ourselves (1 Peter 5:6). Benedict has done a great service with his image of the ladder by showing that there are practical steps that can be taken in order to strike a blow against pride. The rungs of the ladder described stages of development and were seen as pointers to inward growth that had already taken place. They were never intended to be understood as the infallible means of achieving it. They merely measured progress.

The ladder has become an important image to me, not least because it is precisely in this area of behavioural spirituality that I have found my evangelicalism so impoverished and the early monastic writers so helpful. An appreciation of what monasticism has to offer has necessitated getting behind the polemical attitudes of the Reformation period.

I have often marvelled at myself as I have stood with the monks in their Abbey Church and chanted their Offices with them. As I eavesdrop on my self-talk, I hear the surprised whisper, 'Fancy someone trained as an Evangelical chanting!' Chant is considered by many as the best way of throttling whatever life there might be in a text. I then remind myself that God saves us not because of the label we wear, but because of what he has done in Jesus Christ. What other people think, what other people say, what other people accuse me of doing or believing no longer matters. I have come to the conviction, as I hope to make clear in the pages that follow, that monasticism is a genuinely Christian, deeply human, and biblical movement filled with enduring wisdom.

A MORE POSITIVE ASSESSMENT

For me the warmth, humanity and good humour of the Tarrawarra monks make a welcome contrast to the aggression of those who would throw faith at our heads like a great slab of concrete. The blarney of the founding monks who came to Tarrawarra from Ireland in 1954 can be guaranteed to break down the barriers of uncertainty which those who visit a monastery for the first time nearly always feel.

I think, for example, of a former guestmaster, Father Malachy Mara who, with twinkling, mischievous eyes, would constantly warn about the number of young Australian monks who were attempting to take over the monastery! Standing on the verandah of the guest house, he would point to a group of monks at work in a distant paddock and say, 'You can always pick the Australians; they're the ones leaning on the shovels!' Hilaire Belloc captures the world-affirming qualities of this kind of Catholicism at its best in his verse:

> Where'er the Catholic sun doth shine,
> There's music and laughter and good red wine.
> At least I've always found it so —
> Benedicamus Domino!

This is in no way to suggest that the monks have adopted a *laissez-faire* approach to life at Tarrawarra. On the contrary, they order their life and worship according to the ancient Rule of St Benedict as it had been reformed by St Robert of Molesmes, in 1098 CE at Cîteaux in France. As one of the most rigorous forms of contemplative community, the original Cistercian discipline was strict. Communication was mainly by sign language, and each monk had very little in the way of private space. Still today, at the mother house in Roscrea, home now to some fifty monks, the huge unused dormitory in which the monks once slept can be seen with its flimsy, low partitions that separate the beds. Every cough, every movement, every breath of nearby sleepers must have been audible. Anyone arriving a minute or two late to bed had to take off his footwear and creep along by the outer wall to avoid making any noise. It could not have been easy so much as to whisper a prayer on one's own! The only kind of private space available in the absence of physical space was inner space. All that was done seemed to be rigour and ritual with little attention to the needs of the individual.

The changes brought about by the second Vatican Council have made all religious houses much more real and humane. The first Abbot of Tarrawarra, Dom Kevin O'Farrell (now retired as Abbot and living as an ordinary monk in the community), a sensitive and loving man, recognised the destructive aspects of some of the ancient requirements when applied woodenly to individuals. Religious communities were in danger of a kind of faceless charity that is almost the denial of Christian fellowship. He sought to bring some warmth back into the hearts of his monks, some of whom had carried scars from their more oppressive formative years. A key emphasis in his period as Abbot was the desire that each monk should know himself as unconditionally loved by God. His deep longing was that Tarrawarra should be an authentic community of love, which would seek to approximate more and more nearly to what was said of the Christian communities in Carthage at the end of the second century: 'See how they love one another' (Tertullian in his *Apology*, c. 200 CE).

But if love, as distinct from sentimentality, is to be preserved, there is a need for discipline, and if discipline is not to become oppressive and stifle all spontaneity and joy in a community, there is a need for intimacy and friendship. The farewell discourses in St John's Gospel reflect the balance that our Lord intended for the Church in whatever form it would take further on in history: 'If you love me, keep my commandments' (John 14:15). It has been said that law is to love what a track is to a train. The train and love have all the energy but the track and law help to guide each where it is going. How to keep these two together in the correct balance is the art of all true community living. The genius of the Rule of St Benedict is that it strikes a biblical balance between law and love. So, for example, in administering correction, the abbot should avoid extremes, 'otherwise, by rubbing too hard to remove the rust, he may break the vessel' (RB 64:12). The abbot is not to expect his monks to get to the top rung of the ladder in the first step!

The struggle to arrive at such a balance is not unique to monastic communities. It is one that every believer must wrestle with in seeking to follow Christ. It has been suggested that perhaps a better word than 'Rule', in the context of a life of prayer, might be the word 'pattern'. 'Rule' can sound hopelessly legalistic to modern ears. Benedict's Rule was intended to be a 'free-ing timetable'.

We have all had the experience of going on holiday and enjoying a break from our ordinary pattern. We keep late nights and lie in bed in the mornings. We eat when we feel hungry and we do what we want, when we want and as we want it. That is fine for about a fortnight but after that, it begins to lose its attraction rapidly. There is a real freedom in being back at home again with its known and free-ing timetable.

Such an expression of relief is a longing for something akin to the place that Benedict's Rule is intended to play in the life of a Religious community. There is a widespread recognition today that all Christians, whatever their state in life, need some kind of pattern or structure to their day-to-day living. We should not think of this in terms of a restrictive or harsh application of law as was the case in many Religious communities until the reforms that were implemented after the second Vatican Council. What is intended is not the stifling of individual growth but its blossoming within an accepting and forgiving community.

'WATCHMEN IN THE MORNING'

What the Tarrawarra community stands for is best summed up and expressed in the Offices that take place at either end of the monastic day. Both are usually said or sung in darkness. The final Office of the day is called Compline, which means 'to make complete'. Except in summer, the chapel is usually in total darkness. The prayers and psalms are known by heart and therefore nobody needs a book. All is quiet. It is the beginning of what the monks call the great silence which lasts from after Compline till breakfast the next day. The psalms of Compline express an attitude of trust. Faith is written into verse after verse:

> 'I will lie down in peace and sleep comes at once,
> for You alone, Lord, make me dwell in safety...'
> (Psalm 4:8)

'He who dwells in the shelter of the most High
and abides in the shade of the Almighty
says to the Lord: "My refuge, my stronghold, my God
in whom I trust.
It is he who will free you from the snare of the fowler
who seeks to destroy you: he will conceal you with
his pinions and under his wings you will find refuge."'
(Psalm 91:1–4)

Liturgically, the community gives expression to its faith and hope in the 'coming of the Lord' on a daily basis. As one of the final prayers in the Anglican order of Compline expresses it, the monks in their silent prayer, meditative readings and psalmody are as watchmen who wait for the coming of Christ as symbolised by the rising sun of the new day:

As watchmen look for the morning, so we wait eagerly
for you, O Lord. Come with the dawning of the day...

To a Christian unfamiliar with liturgy, the whole thing might look like a charade, mere play-acting. The most profound response to such a charge is to be found in the recognition of our own humanity. We are not seraphim, who gaze unblinkingly at reality all the time. We have to come at it by fits and starts. Somehow ceremonialising what is true does have the effect of helping us. Left to our own capacity to keep things alive in our minds, we might find that they have sunk into a hazy dimness. The great foundation truths of our faith need to be revivified, not because they dwindle in significance between times, but because we dwindle in our capacity to stay live to them. If this principle of liturgical action were false, then the early Christians would have been mistaken to have gathered on Sundays to mark the Resurrection. The liturgical enactment of 'waiting' for the coming of the Lord brings home to the monks what they say when they recite the Nicene Creed: 'He will come again in glory ...'

In faith and hope, the eschatological coming of our Lord 'on clouds with great glory' is anticipated and somehow grasped and realised on a daily basis. The future is thrust into the present. Monasticism, like the New Testament itself, is very much concerned with eschatology: 'the last things'. Indeed, traditionally, monks were supposed to be already living the heavenly life! Now of course it is readily recognised that the monastic vocation is not better than, but just different from, the many other models of spirituality in the Church. Nevertheless, the eschatological witness of monastic life is of abiding significance. Vigilance is the price of liberty. That is the motto of NATO. It is also the monastic motto. A country at war increases its watchfulness. It seeks to establish a twenty-four-hour early warning system so that its forces can regroup in case of emergency. Monastic mentality has to do with trimming the soul and scraping the sludge off a life that is constantly tempted to turn slipshod.

An anonymous saying from the Desert Fathers emphasises the need for vigilance by glossing a text on prayer from the Gospel of Matthew: 'Do you wish to be saved after death?' an old man asked one of the brothers. 'Go, seek and you shall find; watch and knock and it will be opened to you' (Matthew 7:7f). The old man either inadvertently or purposely added to his comment a word — 'watch'— not found in the text of Matthew. This one word significantly alters the meaning of the biblical text and reveals how the Desert Fathers could reread a text in the light of their interests and concerns. An important element of prayer, for this elder, and for the Desert Fathers as a whole, was vigilance, and he was quite willing to gloss the text from Matthew to make this clear.

The command to 'watch' is one that is repeated often in our Lord's teaching, especially towards the end of his ministry, with the cross in view:

Therefore, keep awake — for you do not know when
the master of the house will come, in the evening, or at
midnight, or at cockcrow, or at dawn or else he may
find you asleep when he comes suddenly. And what I
say to you I say to all: Keep awake. (Mark 13:35–37)

Vigilance is associated with the verb 'to watch' in
other New Testament passages: 'Let us keep awake and
be sober.' (1 Thessalonians 5:6); 'Discipline yourselves,
keep alert.' (1 Peter 5:8). This staccato command
accounts for the fondness in the early Church for the
Christian name Gregory, derived as it is from the Greek
word, *gregoreite*, meaning 'watch'. It is little surprise
that, in due course, Gregory became a popular name for
popes.

There were some in the primitive Church who
thought that 'watching for the coming of the Lord' meant
that they could knock off work, fold their arms and just
sit and wait for his return. 'Waiting upon God is not idle-
ness,' said Bernard of Clairvaux, 'but work which beats
all other work to one unskilled in it.'

Among the desert monks, Abba Colobos thought that
watching meant to sit in the monastic cell and always be
mindful of God. But in the New Testament, the coming
of Christ was viewed as a stimulant to action rather than
some kind of narcotic:

Besides this, you know what time it is, how it is now
the moment for you to wake from sleep. For salvation
is nearer to us now than when we became believers;
the night is far gone, the day is near. Let us then lay
aside the works of darkness and put on the armour of
light. (Romans 13:11,12)

A sixteenth-century translation of the Rule of St
Benedict, chapter 22, captures St Paul's sense in a quaint
form:

They that be first up and ready toward the service of
God shall make some soft and sober stirring with the

sound of their mouths or of their feet, or knocking
upon the bed's sides to wake them that are sluggards.[1]

CHRYSOSTOM'S TRIAD OF COMINGS

The fourth-century bishop of Constantinople, John
Chrysostom (born at Antioch probably around the year
349 CE), perhaps more than any other teacher in the
early Church, gave positive content to what the New
Testament means by 'watching' for the Lord. For this
reason his teaching is a useful key to expounding the
theme of 'watching', not only in the New Testament but
also in monasticism. Because he is revered in both East
and West, and because he attempts to systematically
expound scripture, his teaching may be seen as an ideal
bridgehead between Eastern Orthodoxy, Catholicism
and Protestantism. I am far from being the first to think
that Chrysostom's writings have much to offer by way of
theological peace-making.

Dr Barry Collett, lecturer in history at the University
of Melbourne, has shown how significant Chrysostom's
writings were for a congregation of Italian Benedictine
monks during the heady years of the sixteenth-century
Reformation.[2] The monks maintained that the antag-
onism between Catholic and Protestant patterns of
salvation actually rested upon their common base of
legalistic concern with guilt and justification before God
and that the debate was wrong-headed. They believed
that Greek patristic writings, and specifically Chrysostom,

---

1 Quoted by Dr Barry Collett in 'Here Begynneth the Rule of Seynt Benet:
Richard Fox's Translation of the Benedictine Rule for Women, 1517', in
Tjurunga 36/1989, p.21.
2 See B. Collett, *Italian Benedictine Scholars and the Reformation — The
Congregation of Santa Giustina of Padua*, Oxford University Press, 1985.

could be used to bypass the debate between Catholicism and Protestantism and therefore form a basis for reconciliation. Unfortunately their theological input was rejected at the Council of Trent when Rome finally spoke and the hope of theological reconciliation in Christian Europe was lost. Today, however, there is an altogether different ecumenical climate and the ancient Benedictine summons to listen to John Chrysostom may well be more fruitful. What then was Chrysostom's time like?

The middle and later years of the fourth century witnessed a blossoming of enthusiasm for the more extravagant forms of asceticism characteristic of Syrian monks. The extravagances took the form of extreme castigations of the flesh, such as bearing chains and iron collars and eating roots, grass or wild fruits. Part of the intention behind such extreme practices was to reduce the body to such enervation that sexual temptation would not arise. According to his biographer, Palladius, this was Chrysostom's motivation for taking to the monastic life:

> Being well aware of the fact that he could not be
> satisfied working in the city as his youthful nature was
> bursting within him though his mind was perfectly
> sound, he betook himself to the nearby mountains.[3]

Whether or not Palladius was right in his claim that Chrysostom's own passionate nature could not be properly bridled in the city, we can never know for certain. What we do know is that soon after his baptism in 368 CE, when he was nineteen years old, Chrysostom went to live the life of a monk in the hills near Antioch. Major monastic centres were within walking distance of the city. One of the most significant was Mount Sylpios, which dominated the skyline of ancient Antioch at about

---

3 Palladius, *Dialogue* 5 (*Patrologia Graeca* 47.18), Translated in L. Meyer, 1934.

511 metres. In Chrysostom's day its slopes were 'decked like a meadow' with the huts and caves of the monks.

Four years were spent in the company of an old Syrian monk as a kind of apprenticeship; then later Chrysostom withdrew to a cave where he lived in complete solitude, usual for monks in this early period, for two more years. Illness forced him to return to Antioch where he was ordained deacon in 381 and priest in 386. Later, he left Antioch to become Bishop of Constantinople.

There is evidence that other factors, in addition to illness, caused him to abandon his practice of monasticism. In a treatise addressed to monks, he extols the great Old Testament king, David, as an example of someone who remained in the city and yet conceived a love for God even greater than that of the monks. He concludes that it is solitude of 'purpose', not of place, that leads to love of God:

> For with that sort of disposition the blessed David
> dwelt in the city and administered his kingdom, and,
> although he was surrounded by infinite cares, he
> maintained the desire for God more ardently than
> those who live in solitude.[4]

Chrysostom's experience of monastic life had made him very conscious of the foibles of the monks and aware that self-preoccupation might lead to the neglect of wider Christian responsibilities. His later reflections on monasticism are neither naive nor uncritical and they pave the way for the more stable cenobitic form of monasticism which was to bring enormous benefit to both the Church and the world ('cenobitic' comes from the Greek words *koinos bios*, meaning 'the life in common'). Nevertheless, despite these criticisms, Chrysostom continued to hold up the monks as living

---

4 *On Compunction* 2.3 (*Patrologia Graeca* 47.414).

images of what it means to be 'watchers in the morning' for the Lord who has come and who keeps coming. Throughout his homilies he continually harks back to the theme of our Lord's discourse on the sheep and the goats in Matthew 25:31–46 in order to expound the mystery of Christ's coming in the 'interadventual period' (the whole era stretching between Christ's two comings). He saw the life of a monk as a vivid ideal of what it should mean for every believer to obey the New Testament injunction to 'watch'. His homilies reflect an enthusiasm for the ascetic ideal, tempered by his experience of the monastic reality!

Patristic theology does not 'turn on' many modern Christians. In fact, among ordinary Christian people, it is probably one of the most neglected areas of theology today. 'Why rummage in remote ages,' people say, 'when present problems of thought and practice are so urgent?' C. S. Lewis referred to this anti-historical attitude as 'chronological snobbery'. The shallowness of much contemporary Christian life is its modernity. We readily 'sleep' within our culture until we travel abroad and are surprised by how differently other societies live and behave. An attempt to understand the thinking of another age can spiritually awaken us out of our cultural conformities and the mind-set we share with the world around us.

We are not the first generation to study the sacred writings, and the early theologians have rich and varied reflections to engage us. Certainly, there is much in Chrysostom's many homilies that helps to give meaning to Jesus' last solemn word, 'watch'. As the following chapters will make clear, Chrysostom thought in terms of a triad of intermediate comings of Christ to the individual before his final, general coming in power and majesty. Indirectly he comes by means of the written Word of Scripture, the bread and wine of the Eucharist and the persons of our distressed sisters and brothers.

The ascetics in the Syrian hills were the saints of the people who represented living patterns of Christian perfection. But in watching for the ultimate coming of the Lord in the future they were all too inclined to overlook his subtle comings in the present. Chrysostom saw this deficiency and injected into the monastic movement a fuller understanding of what it means to 'watch'. His teaching on Matthew 25 helped to soften some of the potential extremism of the eremitical or desert monks by emphasising values that were communal and humane. Monastic spirituality, as he perceived it, is not a matter of adopting the kind of spiritual gymnastics of someone like the Syrian, Simeon of Stylites, who kept watch during his thirty years on a pillar! The majestic coming of our Lord was not to be thought of in isolation or abstraction from his coming in the daily, homely, familiar, concrete and often messy texture of real life.

As watchmen, the monks of the cenobitic religious orders continue to give meaning to the dominical imperative, 'watch'. Their stable and sensible spirituality is a challenge to live the ordinary life extraordinarily well. They provide a model of spiritual development for the average person whose desire is to live a life beyond the superficial or the uncaring.

OPENING UP MEANING FOR THE PRESENT

There is no suggestion in the pages that follow that we should seek to replicate the monastic schedule in our daily life. In the world outside the cloister, obviously it would be quite impossible to order our days like the monks with their 'interrupting' sevenfold Office. As a father of five children I know only too well the difficulties of trying to schedule family prayers on only one night of the week, let alone several times each day! It is no easier for the mother with toddlers or the business person with meetings late at night. But if the monastic schedule does not work in modern society, the ideas and principles enshrined in this ancient way of life are more important than ever.

Perhaps it is because of dwindling vocations to the Religious life that the monastic challenge is not as clear as when there were many more monasteries per head of the population than there are today. For modern people, a monastery conjures up ideas of a kind of ecclesiastical museum, recalling life as it was lived in the Middle Ages. Dr George Carey, the Archbishop of Canterbury, bemoans the fact that in the Church of England the challenge of the Religious life is rarely heard. He considers that it is one of the church's 'many well-kept secrets'.[5]

It is my conviction that the monastic way of life still has things of value to say to those of us who are not free or so inclined to go off and assume a celibate, monastic existence. In particular there is value in exploring the single dominical command to 'watch' as it was taken up in monasticism and given a rich meaning in the stirring homilies of John Chrysostom in the fourth century.

In our overworked, overstimulated, overscheduled lives, we tend to move through the world as sleepwalkers, unaware of the Christ who is always coming to us. I write out of the deepest affection for the monks I have been privileged to know at Tarrawarra. Like Chrysostom, I know something of the foibles and failings of monks. I am under no illusion about the human imperfections of the monastic community I have grown to love and admire. There is much truth in the observation that the Rule of St Benedict was written for a monastery that functioned imperfectly. The Rule seems almost to assume that there will be misbehaviour in

---

5 G. Carey, *Sharing A Vision*, DLT, 1993, p.221.

church (RB 52), late arrivals for meals (RB 43) and complaints about clothes (RB 55). The 'monastic ideal' is indeed contained in 'earthenware vessels' (2 Corinthians 4:7). But, in spite of their failures and frailties, the Tarrawarra monks keep on teaching me what it means to walk through life with a barefooted soul, alert, aware and watchful, and only partially at home. As a community of 'God-spotters,' they help me to live in such a way as to expect to stumble across Christ's presence everywhere. Their 'watching' has much to say to the modern world.

CHAPTER TWO

WATCHFUL NOT BUSY

THE THEOLOGICAL STARTING POINT

Bernard of Clairvaux, the twelfth-century reformer of the Cistercian Order, used to tell his monks that prayerful output requires theological input. The imagery he used was very crude. He would tell his monks to devour the word of God, just as they devoured their bread in the refectory. Then they were to assimilate it through the process of rumination, allowing it to percolate through their whole being. They would soon find, he told them, that a response builds up deep down in their bellies and finally bursts forth as a belch. This belch, he said, is prayer. '*Eructavit cor meum verbum bonum*': 'My heart belched out a good word' (Psalm 45:1). One assumes from this that the refectory at Clairvaux lacked somewhat in decorum but that the library and the chapel were in perfect syncopation! And so they should be. Theology and doxology go hand-in-hand or as Bishop Handley Moule of Durham once said: 'We must beware equally of an untheological devotion and of an undevotional theology.'

The theme of this book is summed up in the dominical injunction to 'watch'. It was a prominent theme in the primitive Church because it was believed that the *parousia*, or final coming of our Lord to wrap up history, was near. Our theological starting point is to inquire into the meaning of this New Testament teaching about what the German theologians call *naherwartung* — 'near-end expectation'.

'WATCHING' IN THE NEW TESTAMENT

Albert Schweitzer, in his famous book, *The Quest of the Historical Jesus* first published in 1906, has had a profound effect on the way many New Testament scholars understand 'near-end expectation'. Schweitzer argued that there was a crisis in the primitive Church caused by the so-called 'delay in the coming of Christ'. In many scholarly circles this suggestion is taken as an unquestioned assumption. The claim is made that Jesus expected the kingdom of God to be inaugurated in his own lifetime or very soon after. The seminal text for this viewpoint is Mark 9:1:

> Truly I tell you, there are some standing here who will not taste death until they see that the kingdom of God has come with power.

On the basis of this verse it is alleged that Jesus predicted the end was on the threshold and would come very soon. He erroneously thought that his suffering would be immediately followed or even interrupted by a divine act of vindication that would establish the kingdom of God with a global cataclysmic climax to history. But the world continued in the old way. The sun was not darkened, the moon continued to shine and the powers of space remained on course. No allowance is taken for the fact that Jesus was trying to describe, with dramatic picture language taken from the Old

Testament, something that is beyond present human experience (Mark 13:24,25). It is simply asserted that Jesus was mistaken. When he realised that the things he looked for did not happen he died a disillusioned man with a cry of dereliction by God on his lips.

Further, it is claimed, the primitive Church does not appear to have learned from Jesus' mistake. Rather, the evangelist Mark unthinkingly repeats it. The seminal text now becomes Mark 13:30:

> Truly I tell you, this generation will not pass away until all these things have taken place.

When the 'end' does not happen before the first generation has passed away it is assumed that there was great embarrassment. This in turn, it is further alleged, calls forth the creativity of the latter New Testament theologians. John's response is to develop the theology of the paraclete. The interval between the first and the second coming of Jesus is the time in which the paraclete's ministry becomes the crucial factor.

Luke, in his second volume, the Acts of the Apostles, filled the gap by writing an account of the early history of the Church. It has been pointed out that 'one does not write the history of the Church if one daily expects the end of the world'.

The author of Hebrews reinterprets the primitive eschatology in spatial terms. Faith now is not merely taking hold of what is future but of the unseen present world where our high priest presides behind the heavenly veil.

Schweitzer and his followers are forced to speak of a 'crisis' because they think of 'near-end expectation' in temporal terms. But there is another more profound and more radical theological way of understanding 'near-end expectation'. Professor C. E. B. Cranfield has, to my mind, persuasively argued for this more theological understanding. According to this line of interpretation the key to understanding what the New Testament writers mean by their insistence that the end is near is not that it is necessarily going to take place within a short period of time. It is rather, to recognise, as the New Testament writers do, that ever since the birth, life, death, resurrection and exaltation of Jesus the 'last days' have begun. We are living in what Cranfield has chosen to call the period of the epilogue. Between the incarnation and the End, there is nothing left of comparable importance to take place. God invaded our world in the person of his Son two thousand years ago and he will come back 'in like manner' — but all these Gospel events are essentially one divine act for our salvation.

Under the influence of the Church's liturgical calendar, based as it is on Luke's time-scale of events, we tend to think of the death, resurrection, ascension, outpouring of the Spirit and final coming of Jesus as events separated in time from one another, each with its own distinct significance. But we need to remember that John and many of the other New Testament writers draw into the closest theological association the events that Luke holds temporally apart. For John the lifting up of Jesus to reign with the Father in the ascension is seen in the closest connection with being lifted up on the cross to die (John 12:32). Further, John has the impartation of the Spirit taking place on Easter evening and not fifty days later (John 20:22). The writer of Hebrews mentions the resurrection of Jesus only once (Hebrews 13:20). Elsewhere in Hebrews the resurrection is assumed as part of the exaltation of Jesus to the right hand of God. We are therefore on good New Testament ground when we deal with the whole Salvation complex of events in an inclusive way. The events of Jesus' incarnation, crucifixion, resurrection, ascension and final coming are in a real sense parts of *one act of God*.

The 'end' is all the time pressing upon us but as the second epistle of Peter tells us, it is being held back by the long-suffering patience of God (*makrothumia*), giving opportunity for all to respond to the gospel:

> The Lord is not slow about his promise, as some think
> of slowness, but is patient with you, not wanting any
> to perish, but all to come to repentance. (2 Peter 3:9)

Cranfield points out that there were those who understood 'near-end expectation' in a chronological sense (John 21:23; 2 Peter 3:3ff). But they were cited as examples of mistakenness. Their views were not characteristic of the Church as a whole at any stage. In drawing attention to this fact, he takes the opportunity of slamming contemporary theologians who climb aboard the Schweitzer bandwagon:

> It would indeed have been surprising if no members of
> the early church had fallen to this particular error; for
> the church of the first century must have had a goodly
> number of stupid members, just as the church of the
> late twentieth century certainly has no shortage of
> such people.[1]

Cranfield does not mince his words. It is, he claims, the scholars who follow Schweitzer's line of interpreting '*naherwartung*' who are wrong and not Jesus or the New Testament writers. For the most part, the early Christians learnt to live in hope of Christ's return, and *at the same time* so to live on the resources of the Holy Spirit that their faith remained firm even though his return was indefinitely delayed. Far from being an embarrassing mistake, the thought of the imminent consummation of the Kingdom was an integral part of the primitive faith. God's purpose for every generation of Christians is that they live in eager expectation of the future and final coming of Christ. The repeated cry, 'Surely I am coming soon!' (Revelation 3:11; 22:7,20,22)

---

1 C. E. B. Cranfield, *The Bible and Christian Life*, T & T Clark, 1985, p.124.

and the excited response 'Amen. Come, Lord Jesus!' or '*Marana tha*. Our Lord, come!' (Revelation 22:20; 1 Corinthians 16:22) express this expectation. Because of the unexpectedness of this coming there is a consequent need for watchfulness.

St Augustine summed up the New Testament teaching on the final coming of Christ in this way:

> He who loves the coming of the Lord is not he who affirms it as far off, nor is it he who says it is near.
> It is he who, whether it be far or near, awaits it with sincere faith, steadfast hope, and fervent love.

We could say, it is both 'sooner' and 'later' than we expect. 'Sooner', and therefore we must be prepared. 'Later', and therefore we must be patient. Christ has come once and Christ will come again. However long the waiting takes, it is only 'the gap between the thunder and the lightning'.

It is this New Testament teaching that forms the background to the following chapters and provides the matrix into which the key dominical imperative to 'watch' fits. We are commanded to be vigilant, to stay awake, to be alert. '*Gregoreite*' is a command to get out of bed, to be awake, dressed, ready, like the wise virgins in Jesus' parable (Matthew 25:1–13).

In chapter 3, I will look at the implications for prayer of Christ's going away at the ascension. Chapters 4, 5, and 6 will spell out in positive terms what it means to watch for Christ's coming following Chrysostom's triad of intermediate comings in the course of history. Finally in chapter 7, I will seek to show the relevance of his ultimate coming at the end of history. But first we need to be clear about what is involved in being watchful.

ALERT OR HECTIC?

A distinction must be made between being 'watchful' or 'alert' and being 'hectic'. This is a very necessary distinction and one that the monastic regimen compels the casual visitor to make. The monks' day is punctuated by the ringing of a bell calling them to the Abbey Church for prayer. The bells signify 'when' something is happening. Chronological reckoning is essential for any kind of community living. But the visitor to the monastery soon becomes aware of a different approach to time. The emphasis in this case is not so much on 'when' something is happening but on 'what' is happening. A particular period is defined according to its content, not its position or duration on a chronological line.

Monastic leisure bears witness to that which is beyond time. It says that the believer may already begin to enjoy in part the heavenly time of God's coming transfigured universe. The implications of this will be treated more fully in the final chapter. Suffice it to say here that a few days spent at a monastery will have the effect of calling into question the busyness that marks so many Christians. It will serve as a reminder that we do not live only in the world of everyday time.

At Tarrawarra there is rarely any rush. Nature seems to have installed her own clock on the farm, without minutes and hours. There is always time for a quiet chat in front of the roaring wood fire on a cold winter's day in the commodious guest room, or a reflective stroll in the autumn or spring sunshine. Life is so ordered that there is opportunity to take the present moment seriously as a moment of salvation, accepting the providence of God without anxious care for the morrow. Such leisure provides space for the qualitative dimension of time to be experienced. As with a piece of cloth, the length is not always as important as the texture. So at the Abbey. The bells are not always as important as the chats or walks. There is freedom to allow the character of the event to determine the type and length of time that should be placed at its disposal.

Our modern, clock-dominated, booked-up way of living has taken away the experience of qualitative time. Instead, we are gripped by what the Swiss psychologist, Paul Tournier, calls 'universal fatigue'. People are constantly complaining about how tired they feel. They feel tired when they get up in the morning, tired at the office or around the house during the day, tired at home in the evenings, tired at times on weekends or even during holidays.

Where does this 'universal fatigue' come from? In a very large measure, it stems from the compulsive drive of modern life. Do, do, do always more. The sheer pace at which many live and work results in a growing weariness on all sides. And Christians are no exception. They tell themselves secretly how wonderful it feels to be exhausted in the work of the Lord. Their lives are defined and confined by the squares that make up the pages in their diaries. A misplaced diary is enough to send most of us into 'lost-engagement-book-trauma!'

In the midst of a Decade of Evangelism, Christians must realise that it is no more commendable to be frantically busy for evangelistic reasons than it is for materialistic ones. There is no need to feel anxious about either our material needs or our evangelistic endeavours. We are required to translate our faith into behavioural realities, trusting God to supply our material needs (Matthew 6:25–34) and bless our evangelistic efforts (Isaiah 55:10,11) in *God's* own time.

A study of the apostle Paul's travels may at first sight suggest that he was a workaholic in the kingdom of God. A closer examination will show that this is far from being the case. His entire ministry came under the qual-

because he senses that he has forfeited the opportunity to know some of his children and/or that he is aware of having squandered time that could have been invested in fostering a deeper relationship with his wife. Relational boredom and stagnancy are the poisons of a mid-life marriage. Often there is a feeling of the loss of what some call romance. Perhaps because of a false feeling of the security of a commitment a couple begin to take each other for granted. There may be conversation, but the subject matter concerns bills, children and obligations.

We have no time for other family members if we are busy climbing the corporate or ecclesiastical ladder. Monastic spirituality says clearly that life is about so much more than titles and careers. In a monastery, status is of no concern. It points to the fact that some day we shall be only what we are and no more. In heaven there will be no bishops' thrones or even canons' stalls! The frenetic concern for promotion or making money can so absorb our concentration that there is no time for sharing at the deeper level of inner feelings, dreams, struggles, disappointments and spiritual questions.

The truth is that no amount of success will ever feel like success until we have succeeded at the centre point of life. The ladder we should be concerned to climb is the ladder of humility mentioned in Benedict's Rule (see chapter 1).

Those of us with spouses need to take steps consciously to grow in our marital relationship and not to drift. If we have been married for some time, we need to see that marriage at the noon of life offers enormous potential for satisfaction provided that we take time to talk, listen and reach out to each other. We probably need to inject emotional renewal into our relationship — physical touch, laughter, sexual affection — and all that causes us to grow in self-worth.

Christian family life stands to learn much from the

richness of Jewish family life. For an Orthodox Jew, Friday night is a special night, a religious night, the time to begin Shabbat, the Jewish day of rest and religious commemoration. Many Christian people start meals with a 'grace' or share prayers at bedtime. But we have often under-estimated the importance of integrating our family life and faith by means of simple rituals. Small children in particular love rituals. They enjoy preparing for them as much as participating in them. The Church's year offers an ideal basis for such rituals. Brief family rituals can be devised around, what for Christians, is the most significant event of human history — the earthly life of Jesus Christ. Advent, Christmas, Epiphany, Lent, Holy Week, Easter and Pentecost recall the pilgrimage of Jesus Christ and call us into a yearly cycle spiritually ordered and organised by these events. So, for example, simple prayers during Advent around an Advent wreath can be more than an external rite. It can be a means of building our personal and family faith. Time is brought into a relationship with Jesus Christ when it is shaped by the experience of his birth, life, death, and resurrection.

ALERT TO FRIENDS

Those who are single, as well as the married, need to take time to foster friendships. Augustine once said, 'Every friend is a gift of God'. In effect, he says, 'You may think that it was just a coincidence the way you met each other and your friendship developed, but the truth of the matter is that it was not a chance event but a providential ordering of your circumstances to be at the right place at the right time. So treat each other as divine gifts.' For Augustine, an integral human life would have been impossible without friendship. For him, one is less a Christian, if one has no friends.

One of Australia's much vaunted national traits is that of 'mateship'. And yet it is often a very hollow boast.

The Australian psychologist, Ronald Conway says, 'Australians don't have friends; they just know people'.[2] Conway claims that many Australians can see friendship only in terms of 'usefulness' — 'a mate who knows another mate who knows where you can get it wholesale'.[3] But true friendship is a meeting of minds and hearts. To a valued acquaintance I offer my services and my concern; to a friend I offer myself. Most Australians, for all their talk about mateship, cannot manage this sort of relationship at all and men, in particular, are gruffly terrified of it. 'Indeed,' says Conway, 'most boys are intimidated and rubbished out of friendly male-to-male intimacies with the appearance of their first pubic hairs. The Great Taboo — that men shall not love other men — must be enforced.'[4] War, crises, and catastrophe often make men needful of one another in a way that is not apparent under the normal circumstances of a busy and distracted life. The following moving extract was taken from a diary sent home after the Australian capture of Mont St Quentin on 2 September 1918. Personal and place names have been altered:

> ... Well we took the hill all right but God knows how many of our mates died to capture it. When I was home in Bathurst, you never dreamed that men could feel about each other the way we've done here. When Jim died last week I took him in my arms, kissed him and cried like a baby. I loved the stupid big cow with my guts. I suppose June will think I've turned queer or something but she knows me better than that. They say the old Spartan fighters used to take men lovers into battle. I know we used to laugh ourselves silly when we read about it at school ... men cuddling up to other men, and all that sort of stuff. But I used to sleep very close to Jim more than once in the trenches. You

2 R. Conway, *Land of the Long Weekend*, Sun Books, 1978, p.80.

3 Ibid.

4 Ibid., p.81.

could hardly say we were 'on' with one another, but
it felt good, decent, even grand to be close — not
queer at all. Why didn't Dad or someone tell me that
when I was home? Why did I have to come over here
to this dirty butcher's shop of guns and broken bodies
to find it out? A man needs a woman all right but he
needs a man too and I don't see how you really live
an honest life without waking up to that. It's much
more than boozing together. We've been happily
pissed many times but real fellow-feeling is for the
stone cold sober days. You shouldn't have to hide
behind your grog to show what you feel for a mate.[5]

Friendship depends on ongoing contact but there is
nothing in our culture that makes friendships last. We
live in a mobile population without shared roots. Our
friends are 'friends-for-the-time-being', who can be rel-
ished today, and relinquished tomorrow. It is here that
the monastic vow of stability has something to say to us.
Properly understood the vow is not so much a commitment to stay in one place as a commitment to a community of people. It implies a willingness to 'grow
where we are planted', to accept the human community
in which we live. Without this kind of commitment to
others, real soul-searching friendship is impossible.
Conscious steps should be taken to resist the tempta-
tions our mobile culture puts upon us to flit from person to person.

A person who can grab only a few minutes for
friends will soon have no friends at all. True friendship
requires an investment of regular, leisurely periods in
each other's company. It may mean interrupting our
work schedules or putting aside a prior appointment.
Extended, open-ended time is a key for healthy friendships as it is for families. We cannot give this kind of
time to many friends. Nor do we have the energy. Some
of us can manage time for only one or two really close

---

5 Ibid., p.83.

friends. Others are able to do justice to only a few more.

In his book, *Spiritual Friendship*, the twelfth-century Cistercian writer, Aelred of Rievaulx, said that a true friend is one who is loyal and has right motives, discretion, and patience in order to help a friend know God better. Indeed, says Aelred, God is friendship, and so friendship with the spiritually-minded will lead me toward godliness. There is no suggestion here that a friend is to be idolised. On the contrary, Aelred was clear that for friendship to last we need to care enough to be honest. Friends do not stay friends for long when one of them uses flattery to win friendship. He knew also that friendship cannot survive long on benevolent fakery. If we care, we will be honest and we will give time to our friends. There are no substitutes for these things.

We need to identify our close friends and determine to give priority to these two elements. If this means spending less time with other acquaintances and work colleagues, so be it. The person who has no friends is not whole. Friendship is a gift to be desired, to be prayed for and given time to nurture.

ALERT TO SELF

Our Lord does not require us to be what we are not but he calls each of us to be everything we can be and there is always more room for growth and personal development. The problem is that we tend to believe that what we do is more important than what we are and so we become too busy to grow. Real life and real growth pass us by.

We are told, for instance, that the best of us barely tap a fraction of the power of the human brain. While this is true for people in general, it is especially true for the Christian, who can tap into resources outside the realm of the physical. When a person who is a Christian opens fully to the presence of God, there is the potential for profound growth. As human beings we are capable of change and yet most of us have untapped, unrecognised, and unfulfilled gifts waiting to be brought to light.

Professor Robert Banks of Fuller Theological Seminary in California tells the story of a girl he found weeping at a Christian camp after she had been given a great ovation at the camp concert for a song she had composed and sung. When she was asked the reason for her tears, she replied, 'I'm crying for all the other songs I have not composed.' Many of us have 'unwritten songs', talents and gifts that are dormant because in our busyness we have no time to reflect the creativity of our Creator.

The parable of the talents (Matthew 25:14–30), together with the parable of the wise and foolish virgins (Matthew 25:1–12) and the discourse on the sheep and goats (Matthew 25:31–46), spells out what Matthew saw as being involved in watching for the coming of the Lord. Watching, the parable of the talents makes clear, commits us to being profitable servants. God has not set us on this earth to idly while away the time until it is all over. He has endowed us with certain gifts or responsibilities which he expects us to 'turn into profit'. The Puritan preacher, Richard Baxter (1615–91), composed a prayer to this effect:

> Keep me, O Lord, while I tarry on this earth, in a
> daily serious seeking after thee and in a believing
> affectionate walking with thee; that when thou comest,
> I may be found not hiding my talent, nor left asleep
> with my lamp unfurnished; but waiting and longing
> for my Lord, my glorious God, for ever and ever.

The territory between the self we are now and the boundary of the fully realisable self must be discovered and occupied. Under-realised people are seldom truly happy or spiritually contented. Instead of finding joy in creative service, many get bogged down in busy, meaningless drudgery. We are happiest when we live to the limits that God has set for us. They are not onerous. They are tailored to our unique characteristics but they take time to explore, and they will inevitably involve us in some experience of failure. Failure gives the feedback that allows corrective adjustments to be made. It is for growth. Fear of failure will cause us to live constricted and inhibited lives. God intends us to follow his limits and find in them a freedom to be our true selves.

ALERT TO GOD

There is value in busy people defining prayer as 'waste-of-time-with-God'. That is the way Leonardo da Vinci understood prayer. His great masterpiece, 'The Last Supper', was painted for the refectory of Santa Maria delle Grazie in Milan. He took three years on the work, from 1495 to 1498. It is said that, as he was working, Leonardo spent hours meditating in the cloisters. Vasari recorded that 'the prior was puzzled by Leonardo's habit of sometimes spending half a day at a time contemplating what he had done so far'. The monks who employed him apparently resented these 'idle' periods, feeling that the painter was taking advantage of his contract. Leonardo is reported to have replied to their complaint: 'When I pause the longest, I make the most telling strokes with my brush.'

The psalmist cannot stop extolling God: 'O give thanks to the Lord, for he is good, for his steadfast love endures forever.' The refrain is repeated no less than twenty-six times in the one psalm (Psalm 136). The author wants us not only to understand the goodness and steadfast love of the Lord, but to appreciate and experience this for ourselves. In the words of Joseph Pieper's lovely translation of Psalm 46:10, we are to heed the divine instruction: 'Have leisure and know that I am God.' This kind of leisurely prayer takes time. Only if we are quiet and receptive can we open ourselves to God in this way.

Some time should be set aside each day for this kind of meditation with a more extended time given to it on a weekly or fortnightly basis. Many lay people today are discovering the value of an annual period of Retreat. Attention to God enables us to become acquainted with his voice during our day-to-day activities. As we do this, our lives are simplified because we are able to turn a deaf ear to the external noise and internal clatter. We are less divided and fragmented. We can give our attention to only one voice, and our 'Yes' and 'No' arise from the centre.

Our modern pace of life carries a heavy physical and psychological price tag. For many people, physical or nervous breakdown is the only way out of the impasse. This is the drastic measure that the body takes in order to say 'enough is enough'. A long time before that point is reached, we crib time that should be spent on our marriage partners, family and/or friends, our own personal development and being with God in quiet, leisurely meditation. Watchers for the Lord are not idle but neither are they activists. They are not narrow-minded but they are single-minded. 'I wait for the Lord, my soul waits, and in his word I hope; my soul waits for the Lord more than those who watch for the morning, more than those who watch for the morning' (Psalm 130:5,6). It is such simplicity and one-eyedness that helps to distinguish between what is important and what is urgent, between alertness and busyness.

THE STRUGGLE TO PRAY

TWO MEANINGS OF THE ASCENSION

Before we actually consider the various ways in which our Lord keeps coming to us in accordance with his promise, it is important to take seriously the reality that, in one sense, he has gone from us. This might be called the negative significance of the ascension, the conclusion of Jesus' earthly ministry. Jesus was no longer with his disciples physically and not yet with them as he will be in the final reunion. The ascension is the beginning of the time in which the Church must 'walk by faith, not by sight' (2 Corinthians 5:7).

Viewed from this negative angle, the ascension points to the real absence of Christ from his Church. The parable of the absentee landlord illustrates this negative side of the mystery (Mark 13:34–36). Once 'God' is kicked upstairs, so to speak, he is turned into an absentee landlord. And once he is turned into an absentee landlord, we are half-way to making him an absentee. For that reason, it is important that we do not lose sight of the other side of the paradox of the ascension.

Positively, the ascension represents a different mode of presence. Jesus remains present during the 'inter-adventual period' but his presence is no longer limited as it was during his first coming, to the normal mode of being in one place at one moment and in another in the next. He is now present at every moment of time and everywhere. The ascension marks the transition from the conditions of life in this world to the freedom and unrestricted effectiveness of Christ's exalted life. His presence is richer and fuller rather than diminished.

There are two passages in Matthew's Gospel that point to this twofold meaning of the ascension. One refers to our Lord's absence from the Church; the other to the Lord's promise to be with the Church for ever. Both sides of the paradox are important and if our spirituality is to be realistic, both sides must be taken seriously. The two passages are:

'For you always have the poor with you, but you will not always have me.' (Matthew 26:11)

'And remember, I am with you always, to the end of the age.' (Matthew 28:20)

The promise to be present will occupy us in the remaining chapters. In this chapter we will consider the real going away of the Lord — 'you will not always have me' — and its implications for faith and prayer.

A favourite text at healing meetings is: 'Jesus Christ is the same yesterday and today and for ever' (Hebrews 13:8). It is often used to support the notion that the healing ministry of Jesus can be expected to continue in and through the Church in an analogous fashion. It is as though the text from Hebrews gave some biblical support for drawing a straight line from the 'there and then' to the 'here and now'. Few would want to question that a line can be drawn between the two. But that it is a straight line is much more open to question. Because our Lord is no longer with us in the same way as he was with his disciples, the line is more likely to be staggered than straight. Those who use the text to raise expectations for healing are attracted by its note of continuity, but disregard the context which has nothing whatever to do with healing. Moreover, they overlook the discontinuities introduced by the ascension.

When our Lord returned to his Father, the humanity that the Word assumed was not left behind. It was taken into the divine life. Although the actual event of the ascension remains shrouded in mystery, it is still possible to say that we have, as it were, 'our man in heaven'. But in being taken up into the divine life, the human Jesus transcends matter. He now sits at the right hand of his Father interceding for us and waiting till his enemies become his footstool.

In his divine human person and character he is the same, and so is the effectiveness of his redeeming work on the cross. But to say his ministry is the same, and should be seen to be operating through his Church in the same way, is to fail to reckon with the difference made by the ascension. If the ascended Lord's ministry were the same as the incarnate Lord's ministry, then logically it should be the same in extent, method and character.

That means there should be no limit to what the Church is capable of doing, healing the blind, deaf and dumb; repairing limbs; raising the dead. Indeed, why should the Church's ministry be limited to healing alone, for Jesus walked on water, fed more than 5000 people from five loaves and a couple of fish, and stilled storms?

In considering the ministry of the Church today it is right that the promise of Jesus 'to be with us always' is taken with full seriousness. It gives grounds for positive confidence and victory in the fight against sickness and dis-ease of all sorts. Christians have no need to sing their great victory hymns in a minor key. We must never lose sight of the note of victory and triumph in the gospel. But neither must we fall victim to triumphalism. Faith's calling is to live between the two Matthean texts. Faith is in transit. It lives in an interim period. There are probably more miracles to be seen than many of us expect but far fewer than others, on the flimsiest of evidence, claim.

In this twilight zone of faith the Christian experiences a creative tension between the enjoyment of the Lord's promised presence and the longing for the return of the Lord who has gone away. The root meaning of the Hebrew word for faith is tautness or tension. Faith that lacks this is less than it should be. The tension of Christian faith results from its being stretched between Christ's going away and his promise never to leave us. If one or other of these is thought to fail, the line of faith will sag or snap.

There is always a danger of ignoring one or other side of the Matthean paradox. This danger has implications for prayer. God's silence hurts. Human beings suffer, they look up, they cry, they pray, but there is no answer. The heavens are brass, the gates are locked, the phone is busy, and in the ringing silence they wonder if the promise to be there always was ever made. The Lord's silence is mistaken for his absence. The words of the psalmist often seem appropriate to the Christian: 'To you, O Lord, I call; my rock, do not refuse to hear me, for if you are silent to me, I shall be like those who go down to the Pit' (Psalm 28:1). If we are to persevere in prayer we need to come to terms with waiting in the silence. Otherwise, the experience of God's silence will trail off into unbelief.

PRAYER IN THE INTERIM

The widespread assumption that prayer will bring much 'sensible' consolation can be extremely misleading. Martin Luther, commenting on the passage from Exodus 33 when Moses, standing in the cleft of a rock, beholds the back of the Lord as he passes, said, 'A true theologian is one who is content to see the buttocks of God.' Luther is correct, though it should be added that the 'buttocks of God' is a great deal for us finite human beings to behold and probably as much as we can stand without dying (and is far more than is common in most church life!). Even a glimpse of the backside of God would be enough to change us permanently!

Benedictine spirituality as it is practised inside and outside monasteries is helpful not only in coming to terms, as we shall see, with the realisation of Christ's promised presence in Word, Sacraments and needy people. It also helps in the winters of our lives, in the humdrum and mundane, when the negative implications of the ascension seem more real.

One of the ways in which it does this is by underscoring the importance of work. In Benedict's Rule work and meditation are put on the same level. There is no encouragement here for spiritual gymnastics or pseudo-contemplation. It is the grind of daily work that is to provide the raw materials from which high sanctity is made. Benedict did not believe that we were intended to spend our time straining for mystical experiences in rarefied conditions. He was aware of the temptation to turn the spiritual life into an elixir of novelties or a series of fads. But there can be no waiting for the perfect environment to mould and mature us. It won't be found, even in a monastery! The conditions for holiness will be found precisely in the place where we live and work. Benedict would say to the contemporary man and woman, 'Look at your world and learn to see God in it now instead of trying to find him somewhere else.' Prayer and work are not mutually exclusive.

When we apply modern psychology to our experience of prayer it will often seem as though the comfortable words we thought God was saying to us are really the words we had put into his mouth. From a psychological angle this may be correct. But it's not the whole explanation. We must allow God to be first and last in the whole process. He may, in fact, get through to us by means of something like the ventriloquist's dummy. At other times he may not get through to us at all and we will feel as though we are left speaking only to ourselves via the dummy. Such experiences make prayer seem like a one-way conversation, but those who assume that the practice of prayer will bring them a constant 'sensible' awareness of God's presence are doomed to severe disappointment.

There are certain assurances commonly met with in prayer. We should be thankful for spiritual comfort when it comes but not too perturbed when it goes. Benedict kept the mind of his monks off the rapture by setting them to work. He considered that work was not a nuisance to be avoided but a gift to be given, the very stuff of which true prayer is made.

DISCIPLINE

If we pray only when we feel like it we are probably on the look-out for consolation rather than conversion. We want God but on our terms. The Lord is true to his promise to remain with us always. The experience of that promise, however, often involves the discipline of 'waiting in the silence'. It means also waiting without doubting, not being put off by God's silence. We may constantly pray, 'speak Lord, for your servant is listening', only to be confronted with a deafening silence.

The fourteenth-century English mystic, Julian of Norwich, once said that we need to put up with the way God acts, not making a big deal of the fact that we are called to 'wait'. Prayer can be a negative experience and still be satisfying. The important thing is to realise that prayer does not cease to be prayer when it ceases to be pleasurable. God's silence redirects us to a different approach. The 'waiting' and 'silent watching' can be full of positive content. It can be formative. We must simply recognise that God has not ceased to work on us. By leaving us without a 'word' he is already forming us. God's priority is character rather than kicks, and stark, empty prayer is often more creative of Christian character than any of the technicolour extravaganzas that pass for worship in a generation that craves novelty.

Fr Michael Hollings, an English writer on priestly spirituality, speaks of 'hours of dull, knee-aching, waste-of-time prayer'. St Teresa of Lisieux referred to prayer as the 'battle of the eyelids'. But neither was prepared to allow him- or herself to be captive to every passing impulse and reaction. They knew that nobody easily finds time for prayer. The time must be taken. There will always be something more pressing to do.

Habits are much maligned in a spontaneity-age like our own; but a habit need not be a rut. Repeat an active habit and you grow strong; repeat a passive habit and you grow weak. Most of us are 'soft' by nature; discipline does not come naturally to us. The apostle Paul refers to the Greek games and urges his Corinthian readers to compete in the Christian race with dedication. He adds that athletic prowess presupposes training: 'Athletes exercise self-control in all things; they do it to receive a perishable wreath, but we an imperishable one' (1 Corinthians 9:25). Prayer is something to be worked at, not simply something to be hoped for.

COPING WITHOUT PRAYER

In our post-modern world such a disciplined approach to prayer has been abandoned by many people. Although there has been a resurgence of interest in meditation it is seen more as a means of relaxation than as a way of giving honour and praise to God. It is often a self-centred rather than a God-centred exercise. For others, prayer and meditation are seen as providing a sense of oneness or union in a world where estrangement is rife: estrangement from God, from others, from self. That is why managers and psychologists are so admired: they are controllers. Managers control the external world, and psychologists control the internal world. Both can be used to imply that the chaos of modernity might yet be controlled.

Church growth experts are increasingly inclined to tell us that the most fruitful sources from which to draw for Christian ministry are popularised versions of psychology and business management. Clergy are being told that 'vision' consists in clearly articulated 'ministry goals'. Their professional status is no longer a matter of character or theological skill in relating the Bible to the contemporary world but of interpersonal skills, administrative talents, and ability to organise the community. Ever so subtly, clergy and key lay people can start to think that success more critically depends on plans, programmes and vision statements. What has been termed 'bottom up' causation of human designs takes the place of the 'top down' causation of God and the supernatural. Church growth becomes simply a form of streamlined humanistic engineering.

The issue is not *either* God *or* the tools of modernity such as management and marketing. It is, rather, which in practice is the decisive authority. Only when first things are truly first, over even the best and most attractive of second things, will the Church be free to experience the growth that matters.

If clergy are appraised according to the active, visible functions they perform there will be a mounting pressure to neglect the anonymous, quiet, hidden and confidential dimensions that are such a very important part of ministry. But the confidential aspects of ministry do not easily lend themselves to the typical performance appraisal. The danger is that clergy will be tempted to become managers and professionals rather than pastors, thinkers, theologians or people of prayer. Os Guinness quotes the tell-tale comment of a Japanese businessman to a visiting Australian: 'Whenever I meet a Buddist leader, I meet a holy man. Whenever I meet a Christian leader, I meet a manager.'[1]

The sheer existence of contemplative religious communities stands as a challenge to the Church to ensure that the deep, quiet, hidden side of the ministry is not relegated to the periphery. Properly understood, management skills and psychological insights represent purposeful direction and depth of caring in pastoral work. Both should be regarded as God-given fields of knowledge. Both enable us to help people who live in a society permeated with change and complexity unknown in the days of Jesus and Paul. Both can and should be used in the Church with thanksgiving. They are indispensable allies in the understanding of life. But they are no substitute for prayer. Prayer, whether liturgical or spontaneous, must be central to the life of the Church and the individual believer. This is not to infer a false kind of religiosity.

Benedict was shrewd enough to realise that religiosity is a pitfall to be avoided by his monks. His 'little Rule for beginners' warned the individual monk 'not to wish

---

1 Os Guinness, *Dining with the Devil — the Megachurch Movement Flirts with Modernity*, Baker Book House, Grand Rapids, Michigan, 1993, p.49.

to be called holy before one is holy' (RB 4:61). If they were to truly watch in prayer, they must be real in their prayer. 'Conversion of life' is more important than captivity to a religious system. Such genuine prayer takes account of the following:

1 'Pray as you can, don't pray as you can't.'

This advice of Dom John Chapman is always in season. Our Lord may seem to be silent but that is no reason why we should be. The psalms are a good example of this. The psalms are full of examples of feelings of pain, despair, vindictiveness and betrayal vented on God. The people who are most offended by the anger of the psalms are often people who are fooling themselves about their own level of anger.

Denying reality is a mark of make-believe, not of living faith. Look at Jesus and you see God's face wet with human tears and God's heart roused with outrage. To trust God did not mean for Jesus the denial of the evil and brokenness of the world but the absolute refusal to make this determinative. Martin Luther was quite clear about this. He once said: 'God has not created man to be a stick or stone but has given him five senses and a heart of flesh, so that he loves his friends, is angry with his enemies, and commiserates with his dear friends in adversity.'

The psalmists teach us that in talking to God, punches do not have to be pulled nor words minced. Infinitives can be split and emotions expressed. They teach us that perfectionism is twice as dangerous as permissiveness. We can be sure that God, who created us to experience the full range of human emotions, will never forget our humanness, and we should do no less with ourselves. As St Augustine of Hippo wrote, 'we are tossed on a tide that puts us to the proof, and if we could not sob our troubles in your ear, what hope should we have left to us?'

The following unknown priest's prayer is most precious because it is most wretched:

> I am hurt Lord, I don't want courage or a blithe spirit or faith or hope or charity. I don't want to fight or even stand and turn the other cheek to fate. I want to run, to cringe first and then run and hide myself at the back gate of hell, despairing, flatly wrinkled, like a pricked balloon. I'm hurt Lord. Don't quote Holy Writ to me. Don't even say: 'LO! I AM WITH YOU.' I know all that and it doesn't matter for the moment. Just hold me, Lord — tight-fisted, with a grip like all eternity. You do it, I can't hang on, not even with one finger. I to whom others run for counsel and the hand clasp of faith and hope and charity. Hold on Lord, it will pass, but for the moment, hold.

There are verses in the psalms that will jump off the page and make you want to laugh and/or cry with the love and the pain, of God. Pray as you can, don't pray as you can't.

2 Think of prayer in terms of frequency rather than length of time.

Too often people imagine that if they are going to lead a life of prayer it will gulp up large slabs of time which they don't have. It only takes thirty seconds to say the Lord's prayer. Jesus probably intended his disciples to pray it at least once a day — 'give us today our daily bread'. To use it at intervals is not going to take great quantities of time. According to the Rule of Benedict, prayer is to be 'short and pure' (RB 20). To live in Church, as far as Benedict was concerned, was not necessarily a sign of holiness. Much more important was to live always under the influence of the Scriptures and in the breath of the Spirit. The function of definite times of prayer is not to have us say prayers; it is to enable our lives 'to become a prayer outside of prayer'. As has often been remarked, 'to pray at all times, everywhere, we must pray some of the time, somewhere'.

John Cassian, a monk from Bethlehem, who attached himself for a short time to John Chrysostom in Constantinople, would tell his brother monks, 'sneak a prayer out before the devil knows about it'. If you have large blocks of time, the devil has an opportunity to organise his minions for attack!

Prayer is not to be seen so much as an end in itself but as a quality of life. It can be likened to salt. Its function is to bring out the natural flavour. It is not to dominate the food so that it tastes salty. It brings out the natural qualities to enhance it. It is actually inserted in relatively small quantities. In commenting on the seasoning, a person is not likely to say, 'the salt is just right'. More likely the comment will be about the tastiness of the food. Likewise, prayer is meant to bring out the natural qualities of life. It's not a question of choosing between life and prayer — if life doesn't appeal, we'll have a bit of religion! Prayer doesn't replace life.

In *Murder in the Cathedral*, T. S. Eliot speaks of prayer 'at the corner of the stairs', of turning towards God at that moment when you pause briefly to catch your breath, before you move on to something else.

The entire monastic regimen was intended to be a means of turning the monk's attention towards God many times throughout the day. The monastic writers refer often to the danger of '*oblivio*' — 'forgetfulness of God' — and to the importance of '*memoria*' — 'mindfulness of God'. Hence the day is punctuated by communal Offices in which the psalms are recited and the Scriptures or ancient patristic writings reflected upon. To live a life heedless of God is to allow the spiritual senses to atrophy, and inevitably issues in the death of the soul. And this monastic teaching was a reflection of the teaching of both the Old and New Testaments. The admonitions to 'mindfulness of God' are especially clear in the book of Deuteronomy as the writer pastors the desert community in a period of transition:

Hear, O Israel: The Lord is our God, the Lord alone.
You shall love the Lord your God with all your heart,
and with all your soul, and with all your might. Keep
these words that I am commanding you today in your
heart. Recite them to your children and talk about
them when you are at home and when you are away,
when you lie down and when you rise. Bind them as
a sign on your hand, fix them as an emblem on your
forehead, and write them on the doorposts of your
house and on your gates. (Deuteronomy 6:4–9)

In the epistle to the Romans the apostle Paul spells
out the way to moral degradation. It is the way of '*oblivio*',
of failing to make room for God:

And since they did not see fit to acknowledge God,
God gave them up to a debased mind and to things
that should not be done. (Romans 1:28)

If '*oblivio*' is the way down, the way up is the
reverse, namely, '*memoria*'. *Memoria* is honouring and
giving thanks to God, by turning towards him often
throughout the day and allowing prayer to expand into
our whole life. Monastic spirituality is not a spirituality of
escape, as it is sometimes accused of being. It is a spirituality that fills time with an awareness of God's presence.

3 Pray until you pray.

The times when we most need to persevere in prayer
are the times of feeling abandoned by the Lord. Our
lack of freshness and spontaneity in prayer must not
cause us to quit. It's not a matter of praying until we quit
but of praying until we pray, being borne along by the
Spirit of God.

For some, the use of a mantra, quarried from their
reading of the Scriptures, is a way of coming to prayer.
Evangelical Christians are often deterred from this form
of prayer because they consider that our Lord prohibited
it in his teaching in the so-called 'sermon on the mount'.

What our Lord prohibits, however, is not repetition itself but the repetition of meaningless and 'empty phrases' (Matthew 6:7). Our Lord repeated himself in prayer in the garden of Gethsemane when 'he went away and prayed for the third time, saying the same words' (Matthew 26:44). Moreover, a feature of pious Judaism was the prayerful repetition of the Shema (Deuteronomy 6:4) in the daily liturgy. The psalmists also make provision for the reverent repetition of meaningful words to express thanks or praise. As we have previously noted, 'For his steadfast love endures forever' occurs twenty-six times in psalm 136.

Unlike Eastern religions, a mantra is to be used not to get beyond the Word but to prepare ourselves to hear the Word. Its effect is like so-called 'white noise'. When a stray thought, together with its accompanying emotion, threatens to disturb our calm or terminate our activity, we suppress it best by repeating the mantra. Used in this way it is a form of what has been called 'centring prayer'. It helps us to put aside all the debris that stands in the way of our being totally present to the Lord. It is really a kind of preliminary prayer that many find to be a valuable doorway to God and a means of coming to an experience of prayer as gift.

The choice of a mantra is a deeply personal matter, because it is related to the unique person each of us is and our own needs at a particular time. The 'Jesus prayer', in its longer or shorter forms, was widely used in the early Church and it remains an important part of Orthodox spirituality. It is essentially a form of the prayer of the tax collector in Jesus' parable in Luke 18:13: 'God, be merciful to me, a sinner.' Other sentences of Scripture that have been found effective for this kind of prayer are the words of the father of the demon-possessed boy: 'I believe; help my unbelief' (Mark 9:24); the words of the prodigal son: 'I will get up and go to my Father' (Luke 15:18); or the words of the boy Samuel, 'Speak, for your servant is listening' (1 Samuel 3:10).

The important thing is not only the impeding of mental drift but the positive experience of being caught up in a divine conversation. Part of our problem with prayer is that we often think of ourselves as detached from God and needing to bridge the divide by means of prayer. We too easily forget that our Lord has done that for us. We can never do it for ourselves. As a result of his achievement through dying and rising, Christ now indwells us by faith — 'he in us and we in him'. Consequently, we find ourselves praying 'inside' rather than 'to' God. The Spirit takes our heart in tow and turns it towards the Father (Romans 8:26,27). We thus pray in the Spirit, through Jesus, to our Father. Our praying, we come to realise, is part of a prayer-life that is the very essence of God's own life. We are not the prayerless people we often take ourselves to be. We carry prayer within us, because the praying Spirit is within us.

The ascension does not mean that our Lord has retired from his saving activity. Rather it means that he has entered a new phase of it. At the right hand of the Father he continues in the role of our great High Priest, interceding for his people. The king who reigns at the Father's right hand is also the priest who prays. We have already noted that we are prayed for by the indwelling Spirit (Romans 8:26,27). But we are also prayed for by the ascended Son. Jointly, the Spirit in our heart and the Son in heaven invite us to look upon prayer not primarily as a duty required of us but much more as a gift given to us.

The answer to our weakness and incapacity in prayer is not to be found in new techniques but a new openness to the source of prayer. It will include the need for discipline. Prayer is much too important to be left to passing whims and moods. But the discipline becomes a much more hopeful and expectant exercise when prayer is seen as gift rather than duty. It is this kind of prayer that helps us to live creatively with the paradox caused by the ascension. The Lord who is always present is yet always searched for. Our prayer is caught up in the conversation of heaven. The Lover and the Beloved are two and yet one, separated and yet in full communion.

CHAPTER FOUR

CONVERSATION THROUGH THE WORD

GOD IRRUPTS

In the last chapter we saw that Matthew's Gospel presents the reader with a paradoxical view of the presence of Jesus with the Church. On the negative side of the paradox, there is a sense in which the ascension marks the real absence of Christ from his earthly followers, 'For you always have the poor with you, but you will not always have me' (Matthew 26:11). The positive side of the paradox means that he is continually coming to be with his earthly followers, 'And remember, I am with you always, to the end of the age' (Matthew 28:20).

Most Christians can comfortably admit that Christ came in history. They can also abstractly assent to his coming in the future — that seems a long way off! But the real rub is the potential that Christ has to intervene in the present. For all practical purposes many people adopt a 'non-invasive' concept of the divine — a 'god' who doesn't disturb in any way at all. Such a 'god' is treated like a book on a shelf that may be lifted down when needed and ignored the rest of the time. God is a 'Being-in-inertia'.

But the God of the Scriptures is not lethargic. On the contrary, the most persistent thing that the Scriptures say about God is that he is not locked up in Godself or reticent in relation to the creation. God is not isolated, self-enclosed, or un-related. Out-going-ness, self-expression and self-communication are of God's essence. This out-going-ness of God irrupts in the languages of human life, and the Scriptures are an outstanding example of that irruption.

But if there was an original volcanic irruption as the Scriptures were formed, there have been many subsequent irruptions of grace and mercy in the lives of those who ponder these God-breathed words. They find themselves confronted, not by the silence of God, but by the vibrant, awesome reality of God's spoken word. Again and again, the exalted Christ seizes the initiative to come into human experience by means of this primordial revelation and disclose his presence. John Chrysostom was convinced that Christ comes to seek out his people and to engage them in meaningful conversation as he makes himself known to them:

> What am I to do then, you will say, because I have not Paul? If you desire, you may have him in a truer sense than they. For even with them the sight of Paul was not what made them of such a character, but the words of Paul. And so, if you desire, you may have Paul, and Peter and John, and the whole choir of prophets, with the Apostles associating with you continually. For take the books of those blessed ones, and hold a continual intercourse with their writings, and they will be able to make you like the tentmaker's wife. And why do I speak of Paul? For if you desire, you may have Paul's Master himself. For through Paul's tongue even He will hold a conversation with you.[1]

1 *Nicene and Post-Nicene Fathers* (NPNF), Vol.11, p.551 in Romans 15:25–27.

Christ did not abandon his disciples at the ascension. His word is the pledge of his continuing presence. This free disclosure of Christ through the Scriptures read in the Christian assembly finds expression in a liturgical custom at the Eucharist.

When the deacon stands to read the gospel, a greeting is exchanged with the people: 'The Lord be with you.' The people respond: 'And also with you.' But then, it is as though the human agent, the deacon, disappears. The announcement as to what passage is being read is given: 'The Gospel of our Lord Jesus Christ according to ...' In responding, the people turn their attention away from the reader to Christ. They offer praise in the expectation that they are about to be addressed: 'Glory to you, Lord Christ.' Again, at the end of the reading the people address not the reader, but the Lord who has spoken: 'Praise to you, Lord Christ.' In this brief liturgical exchange at the reading of the Gospel, there is a recognition that one of the modes of the exalted Lord's coming among his people today is in the Gospels read and pondered.

What this customary liturgical exchange makes plain about the Gospels is true of all Scripture. Even though liturgical tradition has not provided for a similar exchange in the case of the Old Testament and Epistle readings, we are to listen to them with no less expectation of hearing the exalted Lord speak afresh. Chrysostom believed that this was one of the indirect ways in which the Church is to watch for the repeated coming of Christ before the final, direct coming in power and majesty at the end of history.

GOD'S CONSIDERATENESS IN SCRIPTURE

More than 600 sermons of Chrysostom still exist, and they show him to be a priest and bishop who was a 'servant of the Word'. As an expositor of Scripture, Chrysostom was like a hawk. For him, every item in the text was valuable and therefore not to be 'passed over heedlessly'. His congregation could count on getting away with nothing because there could be nothing idle or accidental in it. His twenty-eighth homily on Genesis is typical:

> It is worth inquiring at this point why in mentioning the three sons of Noe, Sacred Scripture added, 'Now, Cham was the father of Canaan'. Don't think, I beg you, this detail was tossed in to no purpose: there is nothing of the contents of Sacred Scripture which is spoken without some purpose that involves great benefit concealed beneath the surface.[2]

In this attention to every morsel of Scripture Chrysostom may give the impression that he regarded it as something like a 'fax sent direct from God'. But he is not oblivious to the limitations of the human language in which the Word is expressed. The paradigm that is always before him is the Word made flesh. Over and over again, he urges his listeners to accept the incredible gesture God makes to our human condition by the mundane quality of the linguistic medium.

But Chrysostom's unerring sense of balance would not allow him to draw the conclusion that linguistic shortcomings were an indication of a lack of divine inspiration. On the contrary, they were seen as expressions of God's loving consideration. The word used to describe this is the Greek word, *sunkatabasis*. It has

---

2 *The Fathers of the Church* (FC) V.82, Hom. 28 in Genesis (53, 256B), p.191.

often been mistranslated as 'condescension' but this conveys an altogether false idea of patronising whereas 'consideration' or 'considerateness' is more in keeping with Chrysostom's overall thought. When applied to God's activity through the Scriptures it denotes the considerateness by which allowances have been made for human limitations by the language employed. Any sense of patronising is wide of the mark. It is always a manifestation of goodness and providential care. God's love lies behind the language of Scripture even when it speaks of anger and rage:

> When you hear of God's anger and rage, don't get the idea of anything typical of humankind; the words are used out of considerateness for us. The divine nature is free of all these passions. He speaks this way to make an impression on the minds of materialistic people. When we speak with foreigners, we use their language; if we speak with children we babble away with them, and even if we are extremely gifted, we show considerateness for their undeveloped state. God likewise, wanting to make an impression on materialistic people, made use of such words. For in speaking, his concern was not for his own glory but for the benefit of his listeners.[3]

Likewise, Chrysostom saw more clearly than some modern theologians that the language of 'ascending' and 'descending' was an expression of divine consideration (*sunkatabasis*):

> See the marvellous considerateness of the expressions of Sacred Scripture: 'God went up away from him', it says, not for us to think that divinity is limited by place, but for us to learn from this as well his ineffable love, in that the grace of the Spirit recounts everything in this manner, by showing considerateness for our human limitations. You see, the notion of going up and going

---

3 Hom. in Psalm 6 (55,71A) cited by R. C. Hill in *Prudentia*, Vol.13, No.1, May 1981, p.7.

down is not appropriate to God, but, since it is a particular mark of his ineffable love to apply the concreteness of such words for the sake of our instruction, accordingly Scripture employs human expressions for the reason that in no other fashion could human hearing accommodate itself to the sublimity of the message had it spoken to us in a manner befitting the Lord's dignity. With this in mind, let us never remain rooted to the ordinariness of the expressions, but rather marvel on this account at his ineffable goodness in not declining to employ such wonderful considerateness on account of the limitations of our nature.[4]

This accommodation God has made to the limitations of human language is an expression of a love that is unimaginably vulnerable. If I may rephrase some words of Bishop Richard Holloway to the 1993 Affirming Catholicism Conference, the metaphorical language of Scripture is the way God seeks 'to express the inexpressible, to utter the unutterable, to eff the ineffable'! The unavoidable accompaniment of such love is misunderstanding and/or rejection. That is the risk of all love that is really free. But misunderstanding and rejection is not the whole story. There are also those who wait and watch for the coming of the Lord in the Word and who are ready not merely to be informed but to be transformed.

WATCHING AND WAITING TO BE TRANSFORMED

In the Benedictine form of monasticism the reflective reading of the Scriptures is a basic ingredient in the spiritual diet. The Australian Cistercian community of monks at Tarrawarra Abbey could well be described as a 'community of the Word'. The praying of the seven daily Offices involves assimilating the psalms and sentences

---

4 FC, V.87 Hom. 60 in Genesis (54, 521B), pp.179, 180.

from the Bible. Through such regular use in the liturgy, the promises, invitations, demands and hopes of God become part of the 'mind-set' of the monk, ready to be drawn on at any time. In addition to the seven public Offices the monk is expected to spend some time privately each day in *lectio divina*, the prayerful reading of the Scriptures or some other helpful book on the spiritual life. Recognition is given to the fact that the Bible is a big book — in fact, a collection of books. If they are to be taken seriously they need to be read regularly. One way or another the monks find themselves dipping into them many times each day.

The sixteenth-century Reformers would have preferred to have seen longer readings than the short sentences that are used in some of the monastic Offices. The English Reformer, Thomas Cranmer, made provision for the reading of sizeable portions of both Testaments. Only then, he believed, could the parts of Scripture be appreciated properly. He would no more approve the modern habit of setting a maximum of about twenty-five verses as a weekly diet than he did of the little chunks used in the medieval monastic Office books. He had a profound 'catholic consciousness' about the importance of the whole story of God's dealings with humankind.

The length of the lectionary readings was one thing. The method of reading was another. Here Cranmer was at one with the early monastic liturgists in their meditative approach. He desired that the Scriptures should be read in such a way as to allow them to be a vehicle of transformation rather than mere information. His approach was not dissimilar to the method of *lectio divina*.

Although any book can be used that faithfully reflects the teaching of the Scriptures, the Scriptures themselves are the *lectio* books par excellence. Correct teaching was of concern to Cranmer but he, like the monastic writers, saw the primary purpose of the Scriptures in terms of being a 'life shaper', building up healthy and holy lives as well as informed minds. His concern was that Christian people should 'walk their talk'.

It has been pointed out that the words, 'Feed upon him in your hearts by faith, with thanksgiving' could be Cranmer's exhortation before reading the Scriptures as well as before receiving Holy Communion. In his approach to 'sacramental' feeding on the Scriptures, Cranmer has given to generations of Anglicans something of the monastic heritage of *lectio divina*. The collect in the Book of Common Prayer for the second Sunday in Advent is the quintessential expression of this approach:

> Blessed Lord, who hast caused all Holy Scriptures to be written for our learning: Grant that we may in such wise hear them, read, mark, learn, and inwardly digest them, that by patience, and comfort of thy holy Word, we may embrace, and ever hold fast the blessed hope of everlasting life, which thou hast given us in our Saviour Jesus Christ. Amen.

LEARNING FROM THE PAST WITHOUT REJECTING THE PRESENT

Our approach to the Bible through modern methods of biblical criticism has brought great gain and there can be no turning our back on those gains. We cannot pretend that the events of the last 150 years of biblical scholarship have not happened. It might be pleasant and convenient if we could find a time-machine that would transport us back to the days before all the tormenting possibilities of modern criticism raised their heads. But such time-machines do not exist. We now have a welter of information not available to earlier generations of Bible readers and that is precisely our predicament. Fr Michael Casey, the prior of Tarrawarra Abbey says:

> . . . so much information is available on the Bible that we could pass a lifetime on a single book without ever reaching the end of our investigations. The danger for us is not that we would slip too quickly into non-literal modes of interpretation, but that we would delay such a transition indefinitely — to our loss.[5]

Let us pause briefly to consider two traditional methods, namely the literal and allegorical methods, from which we can learn important lessons.

From the third century onwards, scholars began to isolate a number of different senses in which Scripture could be understood. It became common in the medieval Church to think of four different senses: the 'literal' sense, which was regarded as being unimportant and unedifying; the 'moral' or 'tropological' sense, from which one learned rules of conduct; the 'allegorical' sense, from which one learned the articles of faith; and the 'anagogical' sense, from which one learned of the invisible realities of heaven. Thus, it was held that the term 'Jerusalem' in Scripture, while denoting 'literally' a city in Palestine, also referred 'morally' to civil society, 'allegorically' to the Church, and 'anagogically' to heaven, every time that it occurred. The following hermeneutical rhyme summarises this fourfold meaning:

> The letter shows us what God and our fathers did;
> the allegory shows us where faith is hid;
> moral meaning gives us rules of daily life;
> the anagogy shows us where we end our strife.

In the time of Chrysostom this fourfold approach was in its embryonic stage. The literal approach to Biblical

---

5 M. Casey, 'Silence of God to the God of Silence', in *Tjurunga*, No.43, Nov. 1992, p.13.

interpretation was represented by the school of theologians associated with Diodorus and his successors at Antioch. The other three senses derived from the theologians who associated themselves with Origen and his successors at Alexandria. For them, biblical facts were made simply the jumping-off ground for theological fancies, and thus spiritualised away. Some of their flights into fancy were outrageous and often it was considered that the more outrageous the interpretation given, the more acceptable it would be!

THE LITERAL METHOD OF INTERPRETATION

Chrysostom, although aware of the labours of Origen, was trained in the so-called Antiochene school of biblical interpretation. He was deeply suspicious of allegory and preferred to stay with the literal or intended meaning of the text. He claimed that one could avoid the hard work of investigating the literal meaning of the Scriptures by inventing countless allegorical interpretations.

Yet, as we have noted, Chrysostom's literalism did not preclude the recognition of figures of speech where Scripture employs them in accommodating human limitations. To some extent he was able to avoid the extremes of both Origen and Diodorus and is probably nearer to the modern historico-critical method of interpretation than any Father in the Eastern Church. That is to say, he made a real attempt to interpret Scripture statements in the light of the rules of grammar on the one hand, and of their own place in history on the other.

One of the abiding lessons to be learned from the literal method of interpretation is the need to understand the intention of the original author. To do this every text must be seen in context. The habit of opening the Bible at random to see what text catches the eye is no better than the ancient allegorical method of which Chrysostom was so critical and can produce equally bizarre results. It is true that sometimes a passage of Scripture can 'hit' us like a flash of light. But we must be careful at such moments not to abandon a responsible approach to understanding the text. Our Lord does not normally speak to us by the random opening of his Word. As has been remarked, 'You can get a nylon stocking to "work" as an emergency fan-belt in your car, but that's no reason for advocating that all cars be fitted with nylons.' Such wrong-headed approaches to the Scriptures merit a measure of scorn from modern exegetes.

If we are to wait to hear the voice of God, we must not twist Scripture to suit our prejudice or to conceal our laziness. We must pray over it and pore over it until it yields its message. Chrysostom often admired the precision (*akribeia*) of Scripture in the detail it gives. (*Akribeia* is not the same as accuracy. Chrysostom has in mind the detailed character of Scripture.) The same precision and care must mark those who watch and wait to hear God speak today. They will spare no pains in order to understand it accurately:

> The prophets' mouths are the mouth of God; such a mouth would say nothing idle. Accordingly, let there be nothing idle in our attention. After all, men digging in the quarries let no fragment no matter how small go unnoticed, but on striking a vein of gold they examine every single one closely. How much more should we act like this with the Scriptures?[6]

Chrysostom's high view of Scripture as an irruption of divine considerateness demanded of him a correspondingly conscientious effort in responsible interpretation. The dichotomy between how we regard Scripture

---

6 2,2. Migne, *Patrologia Graeca* 56,95.

and how we treat Scripture is one of the greatest scandals of contemporary Christendom.

The Allegorical Method of Interpretation

But having defended the approach of Chrysostom, is there anything that can be said in favour of the Alexandrian school at all? Fr Michael Casey insists that there is. He has pointed out that at least the motive behind allegorical interpretation was sound. The objective was always to 'build up faith' and to keep referring the reader back to Christ.

Many modern commentators would do well to take a lesson from the Alexandrian school of interpretation at this point. In reading many new commentaries, as Michael Casey tersely comments:

> There will be questions that seem to have no relevance
> to the spiritual quest and do not seem to throw much
> light on the meaning of the book itself. The sensible
> thing to do is turn the page. What you seek is an
> explanation of the text not the resolution of problems
> devised by scholars for their own employment.[7]

The key question that the monastic writers and early Church Fathers asked of any Biblical passage, especially any New Testament passage, was, 'What does it show me of our Lord?' 'What does it say about who he is, what he has done, what his purpose is for the Church and the world, and what is involved in following him?'

Monastic reading has the same goal in mind. For the monks, with their slow, prayerful reading of the Scriptures, there was always the intention to build up faith. They would claim that any reading of the Scriptures that does not bring us to Christ is not reaching its full

---

7 Ibid., p.16.

term. St Jerome could say, 'Ignorance of the Scriptures is ignorance of Christ.' By the same token, knowledge of Scriptures brings knowledge of Christ, for the Scriptures bear witness to him and show us how to live in relationship to him.

Monastic spirituality took the words of the author of the fourth Gospel with the utmost seriousness and applied them to the whole Bible — 'But these are written so that you may come to believe that Jesus is the Messiah, the Son of God, and that through believing you may have life in his name' (John 20:31). The object of the Bible is to engender or deepen faith in and obedience to Jesus Christ. So in using it as the source for 'lectio divina' or 'holy reading' the monks were not doing something inherently problematic — something alien to its nature. They read it with a similar concern to the one that motivated its own authors — a concern with people encountering the living Word. In all of this the monastic writers were captivated by the idea that God desires us. They were convinced that it was God's desire that creates our desire. Our Lord was thought of as reaching out to the receptive reader by means of the sacred text. It was a powerful incentive to *lectio divina*.

WATCHING AND WAITING FOR CHRIST TO SPEAK

How are we to learn a more holistic approach to watching and waiting for our Lord to address us through the Scriptures? Many people today are distracted from reading the Scriptures because they have never learned to live by a book. From early childhood they have been taught to look upon books as entertainment. After the casual flicking through of popular magazines, concentrated reading is a new discipline. Even those whose education has involved much reading will often have only the 'one skim-reading' approach to a book. Reading too widely may leave little profound effect, however broadly we may become informed. Informational reading is a search for questions and answers. Logic is important. By comparison, devotional reading dwells more on the basic issues of living before God. It is docile and receptive rather than critical and comparative. Such an approach will, from time to time, incite within us a sense of awe and wonder in the presence of God but at other times our consciences may be stung. This experience of being pricked, pained or stung by the truth is what the monastic writers refer to as compunction. In either case, whether the experience is sweet or sour, one is moved by the presence of God right to the depths of one's being. How then can modern people read to catch the pulse of Scriptures and hear the heartbeat of God?

The very helpful answer given by the monks of the Benedictine branch of monasticism is through *lectio divina*. Von Hugel once compared this approach to sucking a lozenge. The aim is not to swallow what is read immediately as in ordinary reading, but to keep it in the mouth and feel its flavour, as you do a lozenge.

The goal of the process is to find its fulfilment in relating the reader personally in conversation with Christ. There should be a readiness to leave all initiative in the Lord's hands, to recollect and wonder at what he has already done, and to be united with him in living and dynamic ways. It can be likened to the captain of the ship inviting the pilot to take the bridge. For this reason, *lectio divina* is a much more personal approach to reading than many are accustomed to. It involves self-surrender and a willingness to change course.

But there are certain well-tried principles that can be helpful in developing this more holistic method of reading so as to be expectant, fresh and watchful as we listen to the voice of Christ through Scripture.

The need to be objective in our choice of passage.
Michael Casey highlights the value of following some form of lectionary reading. When the reading is outside the individual's choice there is always an element of unpredictability. The reader is forced to adapt his or her thinking to suit the passage set. In this way, there is a possibility of real dialogue between the Word and the person concerned. On the one hand, any comfort or consolation received in the course of such reading is the stronger for being unsolicited. On the other hand, the possibility is left open for a person's life and values to be subjected to the saving judgement of God's Word. In short, we must keep an element of adventure and be prepared for surprises. Our appetite must not become jaded nor our spirit stale.

The need to be faithful to a long-term activity.
When we see discipleship, like the monastic orders themselves, as a long-term obedience, we are more ready to resist the impatience of our 'instant society'. *Lectio divina* is not to be regarded as a source of immediate gratification. Rather it should be seen as the provisioning for life. Fidelity and constancy are its most valuable adjuncts. It is not a dabbler's holiday. As Michael Casey comments, 'it is wrong to think of *lectio divina* as being like a quick trip to the refrigerator for a snack when one feels a little hungry. It is more like the regular meals which constitute life's basic source of energy.'[8]

The determination to remain faithful to a regular fixed time of devotional reading can help us in times of discouragement. Sometimes the Scripture passage read will seem irrelevant to us. Nothing in it grips our immediate attention. At other times it will not be the passage but our own spiritual state that is the problem. The monastic writers refer to the boredom, flatness or

8 M. Casey, 'Seven Principles of Lectio Divina', in *Tjurunga* 1976/12, p.71.

depression that sometimes overtake us in our Bible reading as *acedia*. During such times we are tempted to believe that we are making no spiritual progress at all. Then it is that the faithful continuing in the time of Bible reading becomes a labour of love and we honour Christ in all circumstances.

Such devotional reading not only requires fidelity but it also has its own pace, a slower pace. It is futile if it is rushed. Unlike an Agatha Christie novel, we cannot get through it in an evening. Much inauthenticity arises in our lives because we do not differentiate speeds. We do things too fast. We think faster than we can talk, we talk faster than we can act, and we act faster than we have character for so many actions. *Lectio divina* requires the slow measured pace of regular fixed times of reading.

There needs to be a certain purposelessness about Bible reading if it is directed towards our own needs.

It is difficult to read the Bible devotionally when we know we have to prepare a sermon or a Sunday School lesson from the passages we are reading. We feel the pressure to come up with something meaningful to say. We fall into the trap of reading the Bible as though we were on a scavenger hunt.

For those who are involved in the ministry of preaching there is a need for vicarious listening to Scripture. This is a priestly act whereby we seek to empathetically enter the experience of those to whom the text was originally addressed and to enter empathetically into the experience of those who are now to be addressed so that these can come together, first in the preacher's own person, then in his or her sermon. It is such priestly listening to Scripture on behalf of others that makes possible the prophetic act of preaching itself. But if we are to be nourished ourselves, there must be times when there is no utilitarian value associated with our reading.

Sometimes we may read only one page in an hour, sometimes many. When we feel prompted to do so, we stop and pray according to the inspiration we may receive. We do not read in order to finish the book.

Read the Bible in a way that involves the whole person.

There is great value in reading slowly and out loud, instead of the rapid eye-scanning that passes for reading most of the time. There is an amusing note in a letter from Peter the Venerable, eighth Abbot of Cluny (1092–1156), to a friend in which he says that he has not been able to read his Bible for some days because he has laryngitis! Reading aloud can be a valuable aid in blocking distractions and giving more impact and feeling to our contact with the Word of God.

Singing can be better than saying. Many visitors to Tarrawarra Abbey find that they are better able to pray the psalms when they join the monks at choir in their simple chants. The psalms, after all, were made for singing. The emptiness of the chants is their genius. Like a very simple frame around a picture, it sets the text up and permits it to speak, or rather, to sing. A great number of words might be sung on one note before you move to the next. But the effect, far from throttling the texts, lifts them into the joyful solemnity of heaven itself. John Chrysostom once said, 'He who sings, prays twice.' But chant belongs to the public, not the private, order of things. Very few Christians will want to chant their private prayers, and this is as it should be.

It often helps, if we are the sort of people who are professionally involved in much reading, to have a particular posture for our Bible reading — away from our desk. It is important to create a relaxed and comfortable atmosphere which has an air of stillness about it. In Australia it is highly desirable to use a place that is insect-proof. As Michael Casey has remarked with typical

Benedictine concern for the realities of life, 'a mosquito can do more to destroy our recollection than a whole legion of devils'.[9]

Savour and retain in the memory something read.
From time to time in our reading we come across something that stops us in our tracks. This experience of being 'hit' by a passage of Scripture is quite common. It is a help to write out such a text and spend time, lovingly and lingeringly in the presence of God, with the passage in mind. Writing things down by keeping a journal or simply as diary jottings helps to clarify thoughts when emotions are confused. It also helps to keep things memorable and edifying. The fruits of our lectio divina are preserved when they could so easily evaporate. Sometimes we can turn a written text into a prayer. In this way we are trying to give full scope to a text that the Spirit of God has signalled to us as being of special relevance. Like a silent coach, the Spirit acts within, nodding and prodding, highlighting words from the Scriptures, encouraging us inwardly to move in the direction God wants us to go. The keeping of some kind of spiritual journal may begin to mark the changes of attitude and of our desires before God.

From time to time in this kind of reading we are likely to encounter severe spiritual battles and deep emotional struggles. It will require gentleness of spirit to avoid guilt trips, to sustain enjoyment of spirit, and to avoid being unrealistically harsh with oneself. Such gentleness of spirit is characteristic of the Cistercian spirituality. It requires patience and the long view of our Lord's control of our lives. Bernard of Clairvaux suggested that an examination of the interior life always leaves plenty to be sad and angry about but monks should not always be

9 M. Casey, 'The Pilgrim's Lament', in *Tjurunga* 1977/13, p.354.

dwelling on these things. Instead they should open their minds to alternative thoughts:

> Therefore my advice to you, friends, is to turn aside from troubled and anxious reflection on your own progress and escape to the easier paths of remembering the good things which God has done ... Sorrow for sin is a necessary thing, but it should not prevail all the time. It is necessary, rather, that happier recollections of the divine bounty should counter-balance it, lest the heart should be hardened through too much sadness, and so perish through despair.[10]

The meditative reading of Scripture represented by *lectio divina* is a way of watching for the Lord in one of his appointed trysting places. In small matters that may seem trivial and unimportant, we note the Lord's provident care. In our failures, depressions and recoveries we observe the goodness of the Lord.

What is required is not a longing for information but a willingness to be reformed and a desire to be transformed. No devotional book, not even the Bible itself, can do anything decisive if we are not already longing for a deeper spiritual life and are prepared to receive it. It requires an openness to life-changing perspectives. But if we are truly watching for the Lord, *lectio divina* can be the means of shaking us to the roots. Kenneth Leech has warned that the Church is in grave danger when:

> 'the symbol of the priesthood ... is no longer the altar or even the pulpit but the desk', and when the office becomes something you sit in rather than something you say.[11]

---

10 *Sermo super cantica canticorum* 11.12 (*Sancti Bernardi Opera* 1:55, 12–19).
11 K. Leech, *Spirituality and Pastoral Care,* Sheldon Press SPCK, 1986, p.128.

CHAPTER FIVE

KNOWN IN THE BREAKING OF THE BREAD

'DO THIS, AS OFTEN AS YOU DRINK IT …' HOW OFTEN?

At a quarter to four in the morning the monks at Tarrawarra rise to say the Office of vigils and celebrate the Eucharist. It is this early hour of rising more than any other feature of the monks' lives that causes the modern visitor to gasp. It seems inhumanly rigorous. But as Sr Joan Chittister has commented:

> The difference between us and the early monastic communities is that we extend our days at the end of them. We go to bed hours after sundown. They extended their days at the beginning of them; they got up hours before sunrise. The only question, given the fact that we both extend the workday hours, is what we do with the time. We stay up and watch television or go to parties or prolong our office hours. We fill

our lives with the mundane. They got up to pray and to study the Scriptures. They filled their souls with the sacred.[1]

It must be admitted that often loud yawns are heard from various stalls in the chapel at Tarrawarra but the daily celebration of the Eucharist at that early hour, although not part of Benedict's requirements, is the high point of the monastic day. The closing prayers said in the final Office of Compline on the previous day look to this celebration. The prayer in the Anglican form of Compline best captures the expectant mood in the monastery:

As watchmen look for the morning so we wait eagerly
for you, O Lord, come with the dawning of the day
and make yourself known to us in the breaking of the
bread, for you are our God for ever and ever. Amen.

As they gather, clad in their white cowls, around the huge solid altar made from timber of trees burnt in the Ash Wednesday bush fires of 1983, the monks look to the satisfying of their spiritual hunger in the provision of their 'daily bread'. Throughout the day they will feed upon the Word of God as it is read and savoured in the corporate Offices and in private study. But it is in the community celebration of the daily Eucharist that the offering of their worship throughout the day finds its central focus and meaning. Word and Sacrament belong together as the staple diet of the community. In this way they reflect the primitive Christian communities as described by Luke in the Acts of the Apostles better than many contemporary Churches:

They devoted themselves to the apostles' teaching and
to the fellowship, to the breaking of bread and to
prayer . . Day by day as they spent much time

---

1 J. Chittister, *The Rule of Benedict — Insights for the Ages,* St Pauls, 1992, p.76.

together in the temple, they broke bread at home and ate their food with glad and generous hearts, praising God and having the goodwill of all the people. (Acts 2:42,46,47)

If the 'breaking of bread' is Eucharistic, as most commentators believe, then it would appear that the early Christians celebrated it daily in their homes. There are references in the New Testament that suggest that it was observed weekly in the infant Church on what they called 'the Lord's day', the day of resurrection (Revelation 1:10, Acts 20:7). But whether the pattern was daily or weekly, the Eucharist seems to have been celebrated much more frequently among the early Christians than it is among most modern Protestants. There is no doubt that by the early second century, it was celebrated every Sunday. Pliny, the governor of Bithynia, refers to Christians meeting on a fixed day of the week, early in the morning, 'singing a hymn to Christ as God, and partaking of food together, not however of a noxious kind!' The pagan governor had gained a remarkable half-insight into the heart of Christian worship.

In his major liturgical reforming work, *Concerning the order of public worship* (1523), Martin Luther authorised that the Eucharist should be celebrated weekly, preferably in the vernacular, *as the main Sunday service*. Likewise, John Calvin expected that the Eucharist should, at the very least, be celebrated once every week. He was strongly critical of those who confined it to an annual observance:

Most assuredly, the custom which prescribes communion once a-year is an invention of the devil, by whatever means it may have been introduced.[2]

You could never guess from the pattern of services in some Churches that regular sharing in the Eucharist was

---

2 Institutes 4:17:46.

prescribed by our Lord. People in such Churches often feel uneasy about the repetition of religious rites. 'How can one go on, day after day, year after year, with the same routines?' they ask. 'Does it not all dry up and die?' The answer is that it does dry up and die if there is no taproot of life irrigating it. One can draw a parallel with marriage. The utter sameness of marriage dries up and dies if love departs. But that is not the way things need be, even if in our post-modern age serial marriage seems far more exciting than returning day after day, year after year, to the same spouse.

In a similar way, regular sharing of the Holy Communion was for the primitive Christians, and has been for many subsequent Christians, whether monastic or not, a most important element of their spirituality. In recent times the main church meeting on Sundays in many diverse traditions has become the Eucharist. Increasingly it is being understood that the day-to-day unity of the Church is given and revealed in the week-to-week communion of the people of God.

Other Christians claim that this kind of emphasis on the Eucharist carries with it the danger of neglecting the task of evangelisation. They suggest that if the dominical command to 'go therefore and make disciples of all nations ...' (Matthew 28:19) is obeyed with the same fervour with which the dominical command to 'do this in remembrance of me' (1 Corinthians 11:24) is obeyed, the Church would be in a much better shape. But to correct a flood, one does not want a drought! Eucharistic worship and evangelism belong together. Evangelism is not simply a matter of 'heave, ho, and out we go'. In the Eucharist the Lord sends us out to work and witness in the power of the Spirit. As has been well said, the Eucharist is 'a battle rations for Christian warriors, not cream cake for Christian layabouts!'

But mission is not simply a consequence of the Eucharist. Whenever the Church is the Church, mission must be part of its life. At the Eucharist the Church is supremely itself and is united with Christ in his mission. Mission is integral to the paschal events of cross and resurrection and these events are at the heart of the Eucharist. Too often today, Eucharistic worship and mission are made to appear incompatible.

There is always a danger that monasteries will cultivate a one-sided kind of contemplative and sacramental life that neglects this missionary dimension and becomes narcissistic. Certainly, people have been known to join monasteries out of a selfish concern for the salvation of their own soul, with no thought for either the corporate dimension of the Eucharist or its evangelistic thrust. No deep human maturing can take place unless a person is breaking out of his or her narcissism and learning to become aware of the needs of others. Narcissism and authentic missionary charism are incompatible with each other in monasteries as in the Church at large.

The separation of Religious communities legally, by Canon law, into two different categories of 'contemplative' and 'apostolic', is being questioned by some monastic writers today. Contemplation without the going-out-in-love can turn into religious narcissism just as much as mission without the contemplative degenerates into activism. Religious communities, of whatever ecclesiastical category, are asking how they can make the task of evangelisation one of their top priorities. The answer to that question will vary according to the resources, traditions and charisms of each community. But there can be no denying that monasticism has played a key role in the history of the missionary work of the Church. The Venerable Bede, Father of English history, has preserved something of the pattern of monastic evangelisation in his description of the way in which Augustine and his monks proceeded with their work after their arrival in Canterbury from Rome.

As soon as they had occupied the house given to them they began to emulate the life of the apostles and the primitive Church. They were constantly at prayer, they fasted and kept vigils; they preached the word of life to whosoever they could ... A number of heathen, admiring the simplicity of their lives and the comfort of their heavenly message, believed and were baptised. On the east side of the city stood an old church, built in honour of St Martin during the Roman occupation of Britain, where the Christian queen went to pray. Here they first assembled to sing psalms, to pray, to say Mass, to preach and to baptise, until the king's own conversion to the Faith enabled them to preach openly and to build and restore churches everywhere. At length the king and others, edified by the pure lives of these holy men and their gracious promises ... believed and were baptised.[3]

It is also often forgotten that it was largely from religious communities that the tradition of parish missions originated.

A MANY-SPLENDOURED THING

The Eucharist, like a precious diamond, is a many-splendoured thing, with many different facets. No Christian can appreciate all facets at once. Sometimes the communal facet will be particularly strong. In Religious communities this may not have always been appreciated by individual members but it is increasingly recognised as an important element today. At Tarrawarra the corporate dimension is reinforced by the monks and guests standing around the altar. The consecrated bread is distributed in silence and all wait to consume it together as a mark of their oneness in Christ. At other

3 Bede, *Ecclesiastical History*, Book 1, Ch.26.

times, the note of thanksgiving for all that God has done in Christ will be most prominent. The Eucharist will then be experienced as a foretaste and share in the liturgy of heaven itself. As well as this note of greater gladness there is also a place, as we shall see later, for the note of sacrifice. The Lord who is present is the risen and ascended Lord who has battle-scarred hands. His presence 'has the virtue of death in him'. In a World Council of Churches document, the Eucharist is helpfully described as 'a sacrament of the unique sacrifice of Christ'. This phrase keeps the note of cost to the fore in a way that seeks to be sensitive to the teaching of the Epistle to the Hebrews when it insists that the sacrifice of Christ took place once for all in history. (Hebrews uses the Greek words *hapax* or *ephapax* to bring out the 'onceness' of Christ's sacrifice in contrast to the 'oftenness' of the sacrifices made by priests in Old Testament times.)

Given the many facets of the Eucharist it is not difficult to see why Canon Michael Green, an influential Anglican Evangelical, was moved to say:

> The apostolic emphasis on the Eucharist is, then, not
> something I have always obeyed. But I do so now,
> and I hope to go on discovering further depths in this
> most wonderful sacrament of our redemption which
> is both the means of grace and the hope of glory.[4]

A TRYSTING PLACE

For Chrysostom the Eucharist is one of the threefold appointed meeting places between the exalted Lord and Christian people. There is no attempt in the homilies to define in philosophical terms the nature of Christ's pres-

---

4 M. Green, *Evangelism — now and then*, IVP, 1979, p.106.

ence in the Eucharist. One could never imagine Chrysostom being tormented by questions such as 'What is this — this bread, this sip of wine?' as he partook of the sacrament. For him, and most of the early Fathers, the command was 'take, eat: not take, understand'. It was not a matter of logic or chemistry. To cite the patristic writers in support of later spacio-temporal models of presence is to be guilty of projecting back the ideas and dogmas of later periods and places.

In Chrysostom's spirituality the Eucharist was a mystery, part of that threefold mystery to which he repeatedly returns in his homilies. 'Lo!' we can imagine him saying. 'I tell you a mystery. Christ comes to us in and through the "thingly" species of bread and wine.' But the bread and wine are not merely for exhibition, they are to be consumed:

> He has given to us this Body both to hold and to eat:
> a thing appropriate to intense love. For those whom
> we kiss vehemently, we often bite with our teeth ...
> Even so Christ has given his flesh to fill us, drawing
> us on to greater love.[5]

God knows that for human beings words are seldom enough, especially when we are all aching for reassurance that we are really wanted, we are really accepted, we are really loved. How do we get such assurance, how do we ever get to believe it on the inside? We know that in ordinary human relationships a single touch or hug often means far more to us than any words could express. I can imagine Chrysostom assuring his congregation, 'God knows that there is a need for physical reassurance in our relationship with him too.'

It is very easy for us to 'intellectualise' his coming in the Word and to 'spiritualise' his coming in the Eucharist. But Chrysostom will have none of this. For

---

5 NPNF, Vol.12, Hom. 24, p.143 on 1 Corinthians 10:13.

him, a spiritual presence is less than a personal presence. As a personal presence God makes himself 'findable' to us in the Eucharist. It is his place of appointment or rendezvous. God made us incarnate; God became incarnate to save us; and in the Eucharist, God is incarnate for us still.

Chrysostom was content to leave it at that. Later scholars were to make further inquiry in an attempt to define what he and other early theologians treated with great reserve. What those later scholars often overlooked was that any theory of presence could never be anything more than an approximation. Further definition tended in fact to trivialise what Chrysostom saw as a profound mystery.

THE LANGUAGE OF SCRIPTURE

In an effort to get behind the emotive period of the sixteenth-century debates, more attention has been paid in ecumenical discussions to the earlier period of sacramental thought. Agreed documents on the Eucharist, such as The Final Report of the first Anglican Roman Catholic International Commission (ARCIC), challenge us to examine whether we are not prisoners of now outdated controversies. They also open up the possibility of a richer and deeper appreciation of the sacraments in nurturing the spiritual life.

As an example of this, I have found the document, *Growing into Union*, produced in 1970, particularly profitable. Although written more than twenty years ago (it often takes the grass-roots Church a long time to catch up with pioneering documents!), this book can be used as fodder for the devotional life as well as stimulation for theological dialogue. It was produced in the UK by two convinced Anglo-Catholics and two equally convinced Evangelicals. The Anglo-Catholics were the late Eric Mascall, and Graham Leonard, the Bishop of Willesden, later to become Bishop of London. The Evangelicals were the then Rev. (now Bishop) Colin Buchanan, and Dr Jim Packer, of Regent College, Vancouver. One critic at the time said, 'The idea that the Bishop of Willesden (High) and Dr Packer (Low) can find an agreed solution is the product of the Mad Hatter's Tea-Party in the Old Mitre Tavern.'[6] The four authors were more confident. They did not claim Spirit inspiration for their work but they were sure that it had significantly altered the Anglican ecclesiastical scene, and that it thus could not but affect the ecumenical one. Their agreements are not novel but neither are they mere commonplace. What they were looking for was the oneness of the Church of God, not credit for original theologising. In the process, the following important observation was made about the language of Scripture in regard to the sacraments:

> The language of Scripture about them is the language of sheer unqualified efficacy. If the outward celebration is performed, then on the first showing the inward grace is mediated. Those who have been baptised into Christ 'have put on Christ' (Galatians 3:27). Those who receive communion receive the body and blood of Christ (as the words of institution testify). The simple expectation is that those who partake of the sacraments are partakers in them and by them of God's grace. If there is an occasional warning, such as 1 Corinthians 10, yet the overall picture is one of serene objectivity and confidence on the writer's part in the efficacy of the sacraments.[7]

There is often a felt need on the part of Evangelical Christians to qualify the language of Scripture about the

---

6 Quoted in B.T. Lloyd, *Growing into Union: A Study Guide*, Grove Books, Bramcote, Notts, 1970, p.4.
7 *Growing into Union*, SPCK, 1970, p.55.

sacraments with the rider that faith on the part of the recipients is implicit. For some, the language of Scripture appears to veer too close to magic. It cannot, they claim, mean what it says. Anglican Evangelicals in particular, find it almost irresistible to reach for one of the 39 Articles to clarify or correct the language of Scripture. They are concerned, rightly, lest the Eucharist be seen as a kind of 'Eucharistomat', automatically dispensing grace. Article 25 states that the Eucharist is of benefit 'in such only as worthily receive the same'. True though this is, it does not and cannot alter the scriptural language of sheer objectivity. The mystery of the Eucharist, like all of the Gospel mysteries, may be held only by faith, even though it, like the Incarnation, Resurrection, and Ascension, exists quite apart from faith, 'out there' in the real world.

The great medieval theologian, Thomas Aquinas, expressed his supernally high view of the Eucharist in extremely realist language but this did not stop him from insisting on the necessity of faith, as his magisterial Eucharistic hymn shows:

> Word-made-flesh, true bread he maketh
> By His word His flesh to be,
> Wine his blood: when man partaketh,
> Though his senses fail to see,
> Faith alone, when sight forsaketh,
> Shows true hearts the mystery.

Likewise, in expounding the passage in the gospel about the woman with the haemorrhage who pushed her way through the crowd to touch Jesus' garment, Chrysostom stresses the need for faith:

Let us also then touch the hem of the garment, or rather, if we are willing, we may have him entire. For indeed his body is set before us now, not his garments only, but even his body; not for us to touch it only,

but also to eat and be filled. Let us then draw near
with faith, everyone that has an infirmity.[8]

But when we return to the actual Scripture references
to the sacraments, it remains true to say that it is the language of 'sheer unqualified efficacy'. 'Baptism ... now
saves you' (1 Peter 3:21); 'this is my body'; 'this is my
blood' (Matthew 26:26,28). As *Growing into Union* puts it,
'the overall picture is one of serene objectivity and confidence on the writer's part in the efficacy of the sacraments'.

Many Christians, alarmed by language like this, dismiss Christ's Eucharistic words with a quip about his not
being a literal door even though he said, 'I am the door,'
supposing thereby that they have dispelled the mystery
of the Eucharist. The authors of *Growing into Union* are
not suggesting a literalistic approach to all scriptural
interpretation. They are simply pointing to a dimension
of the scriptural teaching about the Eucharist that,
because of polemical factors, often gets overlooked. It
needs to be noticed and it certainly needs to be weighed
alongside other scriptural passages. When that is done,
the case for coming to terms with the literal meaning is
strengthened rather than weakened. Paul's sacramental
theology, growing out of a sense of what Jesus was and
did, is so rich and so physical, that it is difficult to see
how he could have thought of the Eucharist as merely
an aid to memory. 'The cup of blessing that we bless, is
it not a sharing in the blood of Christ? The bread that we
break, is it not a sharing in the body of Christ?'
(1 Corinthians 10:16). In the end, we must allow the
realist language of Scripture to have its full impact, not
only on our understanding but on our personal and corporate appreciation of the sacraments.

How? How does an appreciation of the 'sheer,
unqualified efficacy' of the Eucharist have a bearing on
spirituality?

---

8 NPNF, Vol. 10, Hom. 50 in Matthew, p.312.

SET FREE TO ENJOY THE PRIVILEGE

The contemporary Church has been bequeathed a legacy of suspicion and mistrust, of misunderstanding and confusion, so that instead of the Eucharist being a glad united feast it has often been the centre of division. The agreement on the language of 'sheer, unqualified efficacy' puts us within sight of new things that previous generations have longed and prayed for. There is great liberation in a Eucharistic spirituality which takes into account this insight for at least three reasons.

1 It sets us free from self-condemnation.

In Homily 2 on 2 Timothy 1:8,9 and 10, Chrysostom makes the point that the efficacy of the Eucharist cannot be impaired by the human instruments because the true host is Christ. He says:

> I am about to say what may appear strange, but be not astonished or startled at it. The Offering is the same, whether a common man, or Paul or Peter offer it. It is the same which Christ gave to his disciples, and which the priests now minister. This is no wise inferior to that, because it is not men that sanctify even this, but it is the same Person who sanctified the one who also sanctifies the other.[9]

The grace given in the Eucharist does not therefore depend on the worthiness of the minister or the recipients. There is spiritual liberation in allowing this truth to have its full impact on our communicant behaviour. Neither the moral and spiritual unfitness of the president nor the communicants can render the grace offered in the Eucharist null and void. The Gospels make clear that the meal that Jesus shared in the upper room was not a meal for the worthy ones. It was a meal for those people

---

9 NPNF, Vol. 13, Hom. 2 on 2 Timothy 1:8–10, p.483.

who were closest to Jesus but who, faced with the challenge to love him even unto death, betrayed and abandoned their Lord.

I may preach lofty sermons to others and then in my self-talk, hear; 'Great stuff, chum! Why don't you practise what you preach?' The problem can so easily be compounded by the demonic suggestion that exploits the points of failure, moral or otherwise, by whispering, 'you are not worthy to be a priest'. In the light of the 'sheer, objective efficacy' of the sacraments, there is no need to cave in to such suggestions. In baptism we are claimed as God's children. We also need to claim God's mercy and forgiveness frequently in the Holy Communion, and get on with doing that to which we have been called.

Of course, it is hard to keep moving on when there are recurring failures, to start each day praying, 'Lord, help me not to do it today', and to end each day with, 'Lord, forgive me, I've done it again'. We need to be assured that the Lord understands our need for repeated forgiveness. Jesus showed this when Peter asked how often to forgive: 'Then Peter came and said to him, "Lord, if another member of the church sins against me, how often should I forgive? As many as seven times?" Jesus said to him, "Not seven times, but, I tell you, seventy-seven times"' (Matthew 18:21–22). Each time a sin is confessed to God, it is treated like a new offence. No records are kept. Even the recurring sin is forgiven.

St Patrick must surely be the patron saint of losers. In his Confessions there occurs this gem of a sentence: 'The Lord had pity on me a million times.' Not seventy times, not seventy times seven, but a million times. Still he forgives and still the sacraments are channels of blessing to people because, thank God, their efficacy is not tied to the fluctuating inner state of the ministers. To come to the Eucharist full of a sense of self-righteousness and worthiness is to leave no space for the presence of a Eucharistic Lord who seeks us out in our brokenness. By definition, grace is only for the unworthy.

2 It sets us free from dependence on feelings.

In 'waiting' on our Lord to come to us in the Eucharist we can, though we dare not readily admit it, be waiting for the right kind of feelings. We don't want his presence so much as the *thrill* of his presence. While we pray 'Let me know your presence' we really mean 'Lord, let my emotions be touched'. What does such a prayer really say about our relationship with the Lord? Are we really watching for the Lord or for the 'liver shivers'?

It is important to be clear, as *Growing into Union* stresses, that the real and objective presence of Christ in the Eucharist is a belief common to many Protestant and Catholic Christians. It is not, as is sometimes alleged, an exclusively Roman or Anglo-Catholic belief. This has not always been fully appreciated by either Catholics or Protestants. There was a tendency on the part of the nineteenth-century Tractarians to deliberately misrepresent the teaching of the Reformers at this point. One of the gladdening features of the new *rapprochement* is that care is taken neither to attribute finality to the Reformers' teaching nor to distort it. Each side of the Protestant/Catholic divide needs to be sure that it understands the other's point of view.

Martin Luther, for example, was clear that our faith, or lack of it, had no bearing on the reality of Christ's presence in the Eucharist. Inner impressions are just that — impressions. They are no measure of the real situation. In one of his treatises he says that before anything has been done by believers, Christ is already waiting:

> Suppose your knowledge and remembrance of Christ were pure passion, pure heart, pure ardour, pure fire ... What would come of it? What would be gained? ... Even if I practised the remembrance and knowledge of Christ with such passion and seriousness that I

sweated blood and became feverish, it would be of
no avail and would be all in vain. For it would be
pure work and commandment, but no gift or word of
God offered and given to me in the body and blood
of Christ.

Faith, Luther claims, does not create Christ's presence
in the Eucharist, though, he would add, only faith can
appropriate that presence. God's gracious action pre-
cedes our believing response. The divine action can be
likened to the blessing a parent imparts upon a sleeping
child:

> Sometimes you go into your children's bedroom when
> they are asleep. You touch them, bless them and pray
> for them. They receive a blessing but never know it.
> In the morning when they are squabbling over who
> has eaten the last of the favourite breakfast cereal,
> you and I are aware of the blessing they have received.
> The fact that they don't know it doesn't diminish its
> power.[10]

At Tarrawarra Abbey, incense is sometimes used
before and during the Eucharistic prayer which is a
majestic rehearsal of the role Christ has played in creat-
ing and recreating the world. It is modelled after the
vision of the world set forth in Scriptures and sum-
marised by Paul in Colossians 1. The prayer calls down
the Spirit (*epiclesis*), recalls the words of institution at
the Last Supper, and offers the Church's praise through
Christ our high priest (*anaphora*). Incense smoke sur-
rounds the consecrated elements. For some, like myself,
the cloud is a gentle reminder that there is something
here greater than bread and wine. For others, it is a
mere falderal to trigger coughing! For none is it necessary. Christ is present regardless of aesthetic and ritual-
istic preferences.

---

10 G. Howard, *Dare To Break Bread — Eucharist in Desert and City*,
Darton, Longman and Todd, 1992, p.12.

The Eucharist is Christ-centred rather than self-centred. Professor Tom Torrance, retired professor of Christian Dogmatics at the University of Edinburgh, makes the point with superb attention to the christological focus of the sacrament. He says that the Eucharist:

> ... is the sacrament of our continuous participation in Jesus Christ and all he has done and continues to do for us by his grace, whereby we live unceasingly not from a centre in ourselves or our own doing but from a centre in Christ and his doing.[11]

3 It sets us free from sterile academic controversy. Geoffrey Howard, a Church of England priest, made a pilgrimage to Mount Assekrem, 2760 metres above sea level, in the middle of the Sahara Desert, the mountain to which Charles de Foucauld went in 1911 to live as a hermit. At the summit of the mountain, there is a plateau of five square kilometres, covered with blackened rocks. Howard describes it as being more like the moon than the earth. There are several hermitages made from rocks on the circumference of the summit. They command a panoramic view of the broad, dusty valley below. In the tiny stone chapel of this barren mountain retreat, Geoffrey Howard did what felt strange to him. He celebrated the Eucharist, the most communal of all acts of worship, alone. As he was about to consume the consecrated bread, he held it in his hands and looked at it. He could not bring himself to eat it immediately. He captured his thoughts in that moment when he wrote:

> I am not bothered whether bread has become body or whether it remains plain bread. Let the theologians argue. Those issues are as sterile as the stones of this place. All I know is that I look at bread but see God.[12]

---

11 T. F. Torrance, *The Mediation of Christ*, T & T Clark, 1992, p.91.
12 Ibid., p.48.

Perhaps Howard's reflection borders on the naive. We cannot avoid the obligation of theological inquiry. The Christian has a duty to understand, as far as possible, the meaning of sacramental presence. But Howard is right to insist that theories on the nature of Christ's presence are no substitute for a faith that rests on, and is nourished by, what is beyond reason.

Care must be taken to not reduce faith in the exalted Lord's objective presence to something that fits into finite intellectual categories. There is a desperate need to get beyond the interpretative frameworks to discover what unites at the deeper level of faith. A certain liberation comes in our enjoyment of the sacrament when we cease to look for Christ with our eyes and intellects and are prepared to encounter the living presence of the living God.

In 1745 the Wesley brothers (largely Charles) produced a collection of 166 eucharistic hymns. They were apparently intended for personal preparation prior to receiving communion and for follow-up meditation after reception. Such eucharistic fervour was characteristic of Charles Wesley, not only before, but also after, his Aldersgate 'conversion' experience. In these hymns there is an impatience with the question as to 'how' our Lord is present in the sacrament.

The following verse from the hymn 'O the depth of love divine' is typical (no. 57 in the 1745 collection).

> How can spirits heavenward rise,
> by earthly matter fed,
> drink herewith divine supplies
> and eat immortal bread?
> Ask the Father's Wisdom how:
> Christ who did the means ordain;
> angels round our altars bow
> to search it out, in vain.[13]

---

13 L. H. Stookey, *Eucharist — Christ's Feast with the Church*, Abingdon Press, Nashville, 1993, p.166.

Laurence Stookey draws attention to the sophisticated theological humour contained in this verse:

> If you would know 'how', says Wesley, ask Jesus Christ
> — the one who ordained the means of grace by the
> command 'Do this ...' Then comes the humour: you
> can ask Christ how all this can be, but you could not
> understand even if you were told. For the very angels
> of heaven hover above our altars in stunned reverence,
> unable to grasp the great mystery.[14]

The nature of Christ's presence in the Eucharist overrides logic and chemistry. If we are to 'watch' for the coming of the Lord in the Eucharist, what is required of us is that our sacramental theology passes from static theory to something, or rather, someone, dynamically present, trusted and enjoyed. Such a transition requires a certain reserve about how we explain that presence, lest we trivialise it. We are required to humble our intellects. Calvin's words cannot be improved on:

> I shall not be ashamed to confess that it is a secret
> too lofty for either my mind to comprehend or my
> words to declare. And, to speak more plainly, I rather
> experience than understand it.[15]

There is a real possibility of restoring the sense of privilege in sharing Holy Communion when full regard is taken for the fact that the language of Scripture about it is the language of 'sheer, unqualified efficacy'. First, it sets a person free from self-condemnation and feeling that their unworthiness disqualifies them from partaking or presiding. Second, it sets a person free to rely on Christ's real, objective presence rather than their own subjective moods and feelings. And third, it sets a person free from sterile academic controversy which turns the Eucharist into a problem instead of a privilege.

---

14 Ibid.
15 Institutes 4:17:32.

The emphasis that has been placed on the 'objective presence' of Christ can be misleading if we allow it to suggest that Christ is somehow passive, as though the Eucharistic presence were a static thing that can be isolated and defined. The grace given in the Eucharist is not some kind of heavenly substance or medicine. Rather it is Christ himself as spiritual food who takes possession of us and transforms us (1 Corinthians 10:3,4). He is the acting subject who comes to meet us again and again in accordance with his promise. He anticipates all the steps and prayers that seem destined to assure his presence, when these prayers and these steps are, on the contrary, the result of a presence of Christ which has already been assured. Before anyone draws near to the Lord's table, he who invites is there. How then shall we watch and wait for this sacramental encounter? What is the disposition of the watcher? Granted that it is not a matter of pretending we are worthy or looking for emotional uplift or straining to comprehend, what is it?

COMMUNION COSTS

The apostle Paul provides a clue to the answer when he exhorts the Christians at Rome to worship in their day-to-day lives by voluntarily offering themselves in God's service. Such self-offering is to embrace the whole of life but it could be said to be focused and given expression in the Eucharist (Romans 12:1,2). For this reason, many of the earliest patristic writers have no hesitation in speaking of the Eucharist as a sacrifice. In Justin Martyr and Irenaeus the bread and the wine are said to be offered, not as tokens of the body and blood of Christ, but as material tokens of thankfulness and prayer. At this early stage Eucharistic sacrifice carried no propitiatory overtones. That was a later medieval development.

Chrysostom is very careful to preserve what has been called 'the lonely eminence of the sacrifice of Calvary'. He will not allow the idea of the Eucharist as a sacrifice to obscure the fundamental teaching of the letter to the Hebrews which stresses the 'once for all' nature of the sacrifice of Christ on the cross (Hebrews 7:27; 9:7,12,26, 28; 10:2,10).

> We offer every day, making a memorial of his death. This is one sacrifice, not many. And why? Because it was offered once. It resembles in this the sacrifice which was taken into the Holy of Holies. This [Jewish] sacrifice is a type of that sacrifice [of Christ]: We always offer the same person ... the same oblation: therefore it is one sacrifice ... By the same token, the offering of the sacrifice in many places does not, of course, mean that there are many Christs. Christ is everywhere one, entire in this place and in that, one body ... and so, one sacrifice. Our High Priest is he who offered the sacrifice for our purification. We offer now what was offered then, an inexhaustible offering ... We offer the same sacrifice: or rather we make a memorial of that sacrifice.[16]

One of the reasons that some Roman and Anglo-Catholic theologians wish to preserve this sacrificial language of 'offering' when speaking of the Eucharist is that they are concerned to ensure that the Eucharist is approached as a serious (not necessarily solemn) activity of the Church. There is a need to avoid what Bonhoeffer called 'cheap grace'. Commitment costs. The authors of *Growing into Union* give expression to this insight when they state:

> If the sacrament is to communicate to us afresh the benefits of Christ's passion, then we must reaffirm quickly that it also communicates to us the demands of it. It may be good liturgically to express our self-offering as responsive to God's grace (by putting the

---

16 NPNF, Vol. 14, Hom. 17 on Hebrews 9:24–26, p.449.

prayer of self-oblation after communion), but there is no real time sequence to be represented.[17]

There is a tendency on the part of some Evangelical Christians to speak of God's grace in the Eucharist as a 'one-way street'. But the divine initiative of grace never relieves us of the need for response. The Eucharist, it has been said, 'holds together the twin truths of God's grace and God's grief'. Both the liberality and the cost of grace need to be appreciated. God's mercy comes from the cross of Christ to us in the Gospel, audibly proclaimed and visibly set forth in the Eucharist, but it cannot remain what it is unless the suffering and dying with Christ remains the mark of its bearers. For the purposes of the-ological discussion, the priority of grace must always be safeguarded. In experience it is not so easy to neatly disect divine gift and human response. Too little attention has been paid to some important words of Professor C. F. D. Moule, one time Lady Margaret's Professor of Divinity at Cambridge University, written over thirty years ago:

> Despite the utter dependence of the creature upon the Creator, it remains mysteriously and paradoxically true that, in the Creator's gracious approach to his creatures, he respects in them his own image — he treats us as responsible persons. And therefore the divine initiative, the unmerited grace, never relieves us of the responsibility for response; the illimitable riches of God's 'grace' and generosity cannot be accepted without the most costly response of which we are capable. For the pearl of great price — beyond price — we do have to give all ... Though we cannot *earn* forgiveness, however much we are prepared to give, yet neither can we receive it with-out giving all, *in the very process of receiving it* ... Relationship means (as it were) closing the circuit, so that there is a circular flow of intercourse.[18]

17 Op. cit., pp.59,60.
18 C. F. D. Moule, 'The Sacrifice of the People of God' in *The Parish Communion Today*, ed. by D. Paton, SPCK, 1962, p.84.

Those who watch for the Lord to come in the Eucharist must not overlook this 'circular flow of intercourse'. They will approach the sacrament with a readiness not only to receive a gift but with a readiness to take up a costly challenge. They will not discern the Lord's coming if they casually drop in for a Eucharist as a friend drops in for a cup of coffee. Perhaps there is a need to recover the practice of fasting, at least occasionally, to jolt us awake and keep us fresh to the privilege and challenge of the Eucharist.

I agree with the liturgical scholars who argue that the Roman Catholic offertory prayers placed as they are before the Eucharistic prayer are liturgically out of place.[19] Some would say that they have no place at all. Nevertheless, I confess to an inner itch to want to use them. Not merely because they are beautiful prayers that reflect the Jewish antecedents of the Eucharist but because they enable me to give expression to what I sometimes feel and need to feel more often:

> were the whole realm of nature mine,
> that were an offering far too small;
> love so amazing, so divine,
> demands my soul, my life, my all.

---

19 The offertory prayers referred to are as follows:
    As the priest offers the bread:
P. Blessed are you, Lord, God of all creation.
    Through your goodness we have this bread to offer,
    which earth has given and human hands have made.
    It will become for us the bread of life.
C. **Blessed be God for ever.**
    As the priest offers the wine:
P. Blessed are you, Lord, God of all creation.
    Through your goodness we have this wine to offer,
    fruit of the vine and work of human hands.
    It will become our spiritual drink.
C. **Blessed be God for ever.**

ENCOUNTERED IN A 'DISTRESSING DISGUISE'

HIDING BEHIND WALLS

AND WORDS

One of the most frequent questions put to the monks at Tarrawarra Abbey is, 'what good can you do locking yourself away from the needs of the world?' The implication is that a monk's life is both selfish and wasteful. Even if the question is not overtly asked it trembles on the lips of many a visitor to the monastery. If, as Chrysostom's favourite Gospel passage — Matthew 25 — asserts, we are to be ultimately assessed on our serving the hungry, the thirsty, the lonely, the sick, the poor and the imprisoned, what will become of those who have chosen a way of life that excludes such opportunities for service? How can such a massive omission be justified?

The New Testament makes it clear that private piety,

aimed at some sort of spiritual self-culture, is un-Christian, heretical and a contradiction in terms. Real contemplatives do not spend life staring into space. Real contemplative spirituality must be lived, not simply prayed. It must embrace not only the lives that people live before God when they give themselves to prayer (it certainly includes that). But it must also embrace the lives that people live before God for the other hours of the day. It is concerned with living in or by the Spirit, and that is a matter of the whole of life.

No one can escape the Gospel imperative to care for the needy. Monks hidden behind the walls of their monasteries appear to many Evangelical Christians to be avoiding the pain of serving others. But anyone who criticises monasticism for negligence at this point had better heed the warning of Jesus about the 'plank in their own eye and the splinter in another's'. Evangelical Christians are sometimes guilty of hiding behind words. They have always insisted that God saves by grace. In this they are unquestionably right. But they have tended to say, 'if God saves us by grace, it is very dangerous to talk too much about the works that our life should express'. Rene Padilla, a leading Latin American Evangelical theologian, has said that the Evangelical's eagerness to push the doctrine 'by grace are you saved through faith', has often meant that they have thrown out any doctrine of works. Even the verse, so favoured by fundamentalist Christians as the one that speaks of the Scriptures as inspired by God and profitable, goes on to say that the purpose for which they are inspired is that we might do every kind of good work (2 Timothy 3:16–17). This failure to keep the purpose of the Scriptures in mind leads to a very 'literacy-centred' view of the Gospel. In consequence, Evangelicals tend to be middle-class and often suspicious of social theology. They are apt to identify 'spiritual' with 'non-material' and consequently words are viewed as being more spiritual than things. This in turn leads to an over-emphasis on revelation as propositional.

It is not enough for Christians, of whatever tradition, to know the Biblical propositions. All are called to live them. In the story of the Good Samaritan Jesus would not give the definition of 'neighbour' the lawyer wanted. He ended up saying, 'Go and do likewise.' Action is required, not theory. The outer journey in service is just as important and just as spiritual as the inner journey in prayer and meditation.

HEART ON THE OUTSIDE

John Chrysostom had no time for statues. In 387 CE he was involved in the famous Riot of the Statues. Evangelical Christians would readily applaud him for this. And Cistercian monks would too. They have a preference for simplicity in church architecture and decoration. Even in pre-Vatican II days, Cistercian abbeys were austere in their simplicity. At Yarra Glen the one statue that exists is of Our Lady and that is not in the church but perched outside in the branch of a tree, powerfully symbolic, even if unintentional, of the hiddenness of Mary.

Chrysostom, Cistercians and Evangelicals would probably all have some difficulty with the kind of statues that were prominent in most Catholic churches before Vatican II. I used to find the crudity of the statue of the Sacred Heart particularly off-putting. The physical organ of the heart with a stab wound, a crown of thorns above it and a flame of fire encircling it, is more likely to engender within me a feeling of disgust than inspiration. But until recently, I had never known the meaning of such crude imagery. Sr Prue Wilson, herself a sister of the Sacred Heart Order, throws some light on it for me when she explains that it was intended to be a window into the love of Jesus shown in incarnation and redemption:

> Its very organic crudity said the incarnation was real. Jesus was a man. The heartbeat of the unborn child was his, and when his heart stopped beating he died … It was shorthand for what loving was.[1]

An old German nun of the Order of the Sacred Heart never missed an opportunity for explaining the meaning of the statue that stood in the middle of the hallway of her convent. She would point to the red physical organ of the heart and say:

> You see zat zee 'eart eet is on ze OUTside and zat is what I am for 'im. Zee 'eart on zee outside so everyone know zat 'e love zem.[2]

And the same old nun was just that. Even if the silent statue didn't convey the message she hoped, she did. She wore her heart on the outside. Her explanation would probably not satisfy Chrysostom on the need for statues but there is no doubt that he would have thoroughly endorsed the need for the heart to be worn on the outside. Granted that Christian love must not be hidden behind either monastery walls or Evangelical words, the question remains: 'How can a contemplative community of monks wear their hearts on the outside?' Is there such a thing as 'contemplative caring'? Before attempting to answer this question there is a need to appreciate the Biblical motivation for caring. Why bother at all?

---

1 P. Wilson, *My Father Took Me To The Circus,* Darton, Longman and Todd, 1984, p.91.
2 Ibid., p.98.

WATCHING FOR CHRIST'S COMING IN THE NEEDY

Central to John Chrysostom's compassionate ministry was the discourse on the sheep and goats in Matthew 25:31–46. The passage is impressive for its restraint and sobriety. It does not contain anything of the bizarre fantasy characteristic of Jewish apocalyptic, no vivid colours, no picturesque details. (No crude imagery like the Sacred Heart!) Its purpose is not to gratify idle curiosity or foster a smug assurance. There is no encouragement to indulge in fanciful speculation about the future.

The purpose of the discourse is to direct attention back to the present. It is in the here and now that the disciples are to watch for the coming of their Lord in his 'distressing disguise' (as Mother Teresa puts it). In the judgement scene, those who think that they are meeting their Judge for the first time learn that they have actually been meeting the king during the whole course of their lives — without recognising him. 'Watching' for the coming of the Lord is no way to escape the suffering of the world. It is certainly not a matter of sitting down and twiddling thumbs until the last trumpet sounds! True 'watching' takes us right into the midst of the pain. Our Lord keeps coming to us not only in bread and wine and the word, but in slum and trench and brothel. The universe has been so constituted that if we would engage ourselves with Christ then we must also engage ourselves with our neighbour.

Chrysostom acquired a reputation as the 'golden mouthed' preacher of the early Church. So constrained was he to preach that he could say: 'Preaching makes me healthy; as soon as I open my mouth, all tiredness is gone!' But Chrysostom knew that a 'golden mouth' availed little unless it belonged to a 'golden man'. He was morally earnest and actively involved in works of mercy. In fourth-century Constantinople, there was a massive gap between rich and poor.

> And Christ indeed has nowhere to lodge, but goes about as a stranger, and naked, and hungry, and you set up houses out of town, and baths, and terraces, and chambers without number, in thoughtless vanity: and to Christ you give not even a share of a little hut, while for daws and vultures you deck out upper chambers. What can be worse than such insanity as this?[3]

While the homeless poor were sleeping on straw in colonnades along the streets, hungry and cold, there were in Chrysostom's flock people who possessed great wealth in houses, lands and slaves. The motivation for social action sprang from Chrysostom's grasp of what he understood to be the mystery of Christ's presence in the needy:

> Would you do honour to Christ's body? Neglect him not when naked; do not neglect him perishing outside with cold and nakedness, while you honour him in silk garments. For he that said, 'This is my body', and by his word confirmed the fact, is the same person who said, 'you saw me hungry, and did not feed me', and 'inasmuch as you did it not to one of the least of these, you did it not to me'.[4]

The Eucharist, Chrysostom urges upon his flock, is not an act in a vacuum. It brings together all that we are outside formal worship and it sends us out from our worship to express what we have experienced in our worship. How can we share the Eucharist if we are not prepared to share our lives outside our worship? How dare we drink from the same cup if we are not willing to drink the cup of common experience? Sharing the cup on Sunday morning is a blasphemy if I cannot share the cup of experience with the people our Lord loves.

---

3 NPNF, Vol.11, Hom.14 in Romans, p.452.
4 NPNF. Vol.10, Hom.50 in Matthew, p.313.

We are not called to love Christ in the abstract, but to recognise him in the manifold ways in which he comes to us. Because Chrysostom was convinced that our Lord meets us incognito in the needy, he stresses the privilege that is given to the rich in serving the poor:

> Make yourself a guest-chamber in your own house:
> set up a bed there, set up a table there and a candle-
> stick ... Have a room to which Christ may come. Say,
> 'This is Christ's cell: this building is set apart for him.'
> Even though it is just a little insignificant room in the
> basement, he does not disdain it. Naked and a
> stranger, Christ goes about — all he wants is shelter.
> Make it available even though it is as little as this.[5]

The New Testament provides many different incentives for Christians to spend and be spent in the service of their distressed brothers and sisters. There is the eschatological incentive, with the emphasis on rewards and punishments. We see something of that in this discourse with the 'Come, you that are blessed by my Father, inherit the kingdom prepared for you from the foundation of the world' (Matthew 25:34), and 'You that are accursed, depart from me into the eternal fire prepared for the devil and his angels' (Matthew 25:41). As well as the eschatological incentive there is the incentive that arises from a consideration of all that God has done for us through Christ on Calvary's cross. 'For the love of Christ urges us on, because we are convinced that one has died for all; therefore all have died. And he died for all, so that those who live might live no longer for themselves, but for him who died and was raised for them' (2 Corinthians 5:14). But in addition to the incentives for compassionate service that arise from a consideration of what lies ahead and what lies behind there is the powerful incentive in the mystery that confronts us in the present.

---

5 NPNF, Vol.11, Hom.40 in Acts, pp.245ff.

Not all New Testament scholars would go along with Chrysostom in seeing the disclosure of a mystery in this passage. Some see this passage as referring to the presence of Christ in needy believers only. Christ indwells believers through his Spirit. In that case, it is claimed, the passage must be set in the context of the mission of the disciples. Their commission was to go from town to town preaching the Gospel and Jesus promised, 'Whoever welcomes you welcomes me' (Matthew 10:40). According to this view, Jesus would be present in his representatives, namely, the disciples.

The difficulty with this interpretation is that it makes the compassionate offering of hospitality to Christians the universal criterion for final judgement and this means that entire populations will be condemned, for there are millions who never get the chance of succouring a needy Christian. When Jesus refers to 'just as you did not do it to one of the least of these, you did not do it to me' (Matthew 25:45), he means the needy generally, irrespective of whether they are Christ's disciples. The discourse is about the judgement of all, including Christians, according to their treatment of their needy neighbours regardless of race, sex or creed.

What Jesus discloses in this passage is that, just as he is present in his freedom and lordship in the Scriptures read and heard and in the Holy Supper by means of the bread and wine, so he meets us in all whom we serve, not because of our serving, but as a matter of his free and royal decision. It is as sure as his grace but it is something over which we have no power.

To know this mystery is to know that in our service of the needy all thought of patronising is once for all excluded. There can be no place for put-downs or one-upmanship in our serving. To serve the hungry, thirsty, poor, sick and imprisoned is to do more than simply respond to the Gospel with specific acts of kindness. It is to offer a very direct personal service to the exalted

Lord himself. How could we feel ourselves superior to the one who comes with his majesty clothed in power-lessness? A realisation of the mystery disclosed in this discourse has the effect of giving birth to a disturbing dissatisfaction with the middle-class interpretation of the Gospels which many Christians have imbibed for most of their lives. It calls for a radical renewal of life-style. By drawing near in the persons of the needy, Jesus is the embodiment or sacrament of the accessible, and therefore vulnerable, God. To 'watch' for his coming is the very reverse of folding our arms and legs and with-drawing from the suffering of the world. Rather it requires that we show that same risky, vulnerable love as the One whose arms and legs were tortured and twisted on a cross.

Jim Wallis is a Christian activist and founder of the Sojourners community in Washington DC. His commu-nity seeks to minister to the homeless people who shel-ter in cardboard boxes against the pipes that spew out the exhaust from the White House heating system. The community has a kitchen in which they serve meals to the people who queue every day to get something to eat. On one occasion Jim asked Mary Glover, an Afro-American volunteer, to pray for the waiting queue before the doors were opened:

'Lord,' she prayed, 'we know that you will be comin' down this line today, so help us to treat you real good.'

It was a heartfelt expression of the same conviction that drove John Chrysostom to address the social needs of the fourth century. His understanding of Matthew 25 would not allow him to do otherwise. In the light of this profound passage what can we say to the question with which this chapter began? What, if anything, have con-templative communities such as Tarrawarra to say about the nature of Christian service? What might 'contemplative caring' have to say to the wider Christian community today? How can it stir us to have more of a cutting edge in our ministry of service, especially to the poor and those who suffer unjustly?

CONTEMPLATIVE CARING

'Contemplative caring' may be defined as the kind of care that seeks to strike a balance between 'being' and 'doing'. Many social activists derive an inner pleasure from immersing themselves among the poor. Because the need is bottomless ('the poor you have with you always'), they often suffer burn-out. We are better able to watch for the coming of Christ when we cease from frenetic activity in our own strength. As St Augustine wrote:

> We shall rest and we shall see.
> We shall see and we shall love.
> We shall love and we shall praise.

Until we rest, we cannot see. Until we see, we cannot love. Until we love, we cannot praise. Rest, prayer and contemplation are indispensable to a ministry of compassion. Monastic communities bear witness to, and help to foster, this 'contemplative caring' in a number of ways.

HOSPITALITY

According to the Rule of Benedict 'all guests are to be received as Christ' (RB 53). We must note the word 'all'. Even those who are not 'our kind of folk' are to be received as Christ. This reflects both the teaching and example of Jesus. He was nicknamed by the respectable religious leaders, 'friend of sinners'. He implied in his teaching that the offer of hospitality to those who can repay it is no pointer to the gospel of undeserved grace (Luke 14:12–14). There is nothing characteristically Christian in showing hospitality to those whose company we find personally congenial.

In the modern world, the biblical value of hospitality is reduced to one of the social graces — the affluent reception of the affluent — rather than being a pointer to God's mercy in Christ. Unless a beginning is made to applying the Benedictine principle of hospitality in our own homes, the world will become a colder and more heartless place for those who are isolated on the margins of society.

The teaching of Jesus echoed in Benedict may strike us as idealistic and impracticable but the Rule is sensible. It requires that the community should greet the guests but not linger talking to them. In other words, Benedict would not allow hospitality to become an excuse for lack of organisation.

Most monastic communities generally manage to preserve the integrity of their way of life and generously share something of it with others. Sharing is the key. Hospitality is not about abundance but about sharing. There is a never-ending trickle of visitors who come to stay in Abbey guest-houses where the traditional monastic welcome is dispensed to men and women of whatever creed or culture. Some are people who have been broken and bruised by the storms of life and they find in the warmth and acceptance of the community and its gentle round of worship a shelter from the storm. This is a side of monastic life that should not be underestimated.

There are more and more people in the caring professions who are finding value in a few days' retreat at a monastery. If the monastery cannot be directly in touch with the monstrous burden of suffering in the community it can offer a very real ministry of 'caring for the carers'. I find that when I am played out, there is nothing like plugging into the life of the community prayer at Tarrawarra. Instead of straining to revive myself with all manner of piety, I experience the community offering its praise and prayer and allow myself to quietly slip into its rhythm.

QUALITY CARE

While the offer of hospitality is a generous and much appreciated side of monastic life, it cannot be allowed to develop into the primary concern of a contemplative community. But the small scale of the caring ministry provided does have the effect of raising the question of quality of care against quantity.

It is too easy to base our assessment on the value of a course of action by using quantitative criteria. Like the apostles who said to Jesus: 'What are five loaves and two fishes among so many?' we are apt to dismiss the small offering. This is to risk depriving every small deed of any substantial meaning. It has been well said that a small kindness done in a caring community can go unnoticed but in a concentration camp it is a symbol of all kindness! Jesus had something to say about the value of the cup of cold water given in his name: 'Whoever gives even a cup of cold water to one of these little ones … will not lose their reward' (Matthew 10:42). Our efforts will often seem like a drop in the ocean of need but our Lord promised that even the smallest gift, given for the right motive, does not go unnoticed. We know what he did with the five loaves and few fish. There is no need to be intimidated by the smallness of our human resources so long as our finite hearts are open to being filled with his infinite love.

To the professional carer, the patient or client is often just another case among hundreds. To the person on the receiving end of such care, it is the moment for which they have made a special and sometimes difficult journey, the moment for which they have been waiting for a long time, the moment of anxiety, perhaps of hope that something helpful will be done or said. But sadly, even the best professionals seem to forget how vulnerable their clients are.

'Contemplative caring' puts the emphasis on the quality of caring. As one pastor has said 'if I take care of the depth of my ministry, God will take care of its extent'. To follow Christ it is not sufficient to serve in the sense of performing the service, getting the job done, rushing around the hospital ward or parish in a 'hail fellow well met' fashion. If we do indeed encounter the exalted Lord in the needy, then we need to look to the quality of the interaction between the servant and the one to whom the service is rendered. The mystery is located in the meeting of persons. The performance of the task (be it leadership, teaching, nursing, listening, visiting or something else) is purely instrumental. It offers the occasion for service and that service will often be a risky enterprise, characterised by vulnerability.

But monastic spirituality insists that small actions may not only be deep in quality, they may also be global in their scope. If we care for our own world, others might be more mindful of theirs. In a world that has become a global village where decisions made in one part have long-range consequences for other parts, the monastic mentality of lovingly tending to one little patch of garden has an urgent sense of relevance. With our pressurised aerosol cans we destroy the ozone layer and contribute to the drought affecting food supplies in Somalia. Farmers with their sprays poison the food sold in supermarkets all over the world. Nuclear tests in the Australian outback put the lives of Aboriginal people at risk for years to come. Benedictine monasticism witnesses to the connectedness of life. Everything is sacred. Animate and inanimate creation are alike vehicles of the holy. When Benedict writes in his Rule, 'regard all the utensils of the monastery and its whole property as if they were the sacred vessels of the altar' (RB 31:10), his wisdom lends itself to wide application in today's world.

SOCIAL CRITIC

Thomas Merton is probably the best-known of all Cistercian monks. He regarded the monk as essentially someone who takes up a critical attitude towards the contemporary world and its structures. From his Abbey of Gethsemani in the USA his voice of protest was heard on issues such as the Vietnam war, the peace movement and racialism.

In the American racial problems of the 1960s, Merton criticised the conceit of whites who thought that the blacks wanted to adopt their values and ideas. He said:

> ... the irony is that the Negro ... is offering the white man a 'message of salvation,' but the white man is so blinded by his self-sufficiency and self-conceit that he does not recognise the peril in which he puts himself by ignoring the offer.[6]

The well-known American Church historian Martin E. Marty attacked Merton vehemently for his comments. How did a monk, sitting safely behind the walls of a Cistercian monastery, dare to take on the mantle of a prophet and predict a period of violence? But in 1967, when the American cities were in flames and the Black Power movement had been launched, Marty wrote that the monk Merton understood the situation of his country more deeply and fundamentally than he himself and he offered a public apology for his harsh criticism.

It was precisely in his monastic seclusion that Merton had discovered the possibility of compassion. This is not to suggest that Merton's help was given directly to the needy by his retiring to the monastery. It is rather that

6 H. Nouwen, *Pray to Live — Thomas Merton, Contemplative — Critic,* Notre Dame, p.60.

in his prayer and silence, he came to realise that the evil, sin and violence that he saw in the world, were deeply rooted in his own heart. By casting himself on the mercy of God, he received forgiveness and then gave forgiveness to those who threatened society with violence. His life became an open conduit for love.

But it is not only the monk who is called to be a critic of society. The monk serves to witness to the prophetic responsibility that the whole Church has to critique current social trends. If we are to fulfil this function we must constantly study not only the Bible but also the popular media.

Every day, through television, newspapers and radio, a thousand human needs beckon from around the nation and the world. Global tragedies are fleetingly presented for visual impact and we feel powerless to act. We need to resolve to stand against turning serious issues into entertainment and to try to listen critically to what we hear and think. Instead of switching to another channel or turning the page, we are presented with a challenge to find out what it is about our own lives that could be affecting the poor who live thousands of miles away or as near as the next suburb, the next house. If we are to avoid human callousness, we simply cannot continue to watch people starving to death on the evening news while we eat our dinner without so much as raising our eyebrows. 'Contemplative caring' begins with the timeless question: 'Lord, what would you have me do?'

RESOURCES

Anyone engaged in seeking to address the mega-problems of third world poverty, pollution, or racialism soon learns that the challenges are persistent and tiring. These are enormously complex social issues that will not be overcome by the occasional street march, rally or protest. Each issue deals with questions that penetrate very deeply into the core of human existence and there are times when we feel inclined to cave into the suggestion that any attempt to alleviate distress is an impossible venture. With the constant demands for the expenditure of much physical, intellectual and emotional energy, we soon run up against our own bankruptcy. If the interior life is neglected the Christian activist is in danger of becoming a bitter idealist or a despondent wreck.

Humanly speaking, the Gospel describes a quality and style of life that is impossible. When we read monastic texts like the Rule of Benedict we need to keep reminding ourselves of their implicit theology of grace. There is much moral exhortation in monastic texts, but they were never intended to be read outside the context of the inspiration and energy of grace. Grace and the power of the Holy Spirit is taken for granted. Contemplative caring is not first and foremost a matter of know-how or can-do, but of the presence and power of Christ through the Spirit.

Humility rather than cocksureness is needed because even when such help and guidance of the Spirit of God is sought, the reality is that we remain flawed and very often confused creatures. Thomas Merton saw that the roots of racial violence in America lay in the whites themselves because though many of them were in favour of integration they would only fight for it as long as they didn't feel their own lives, and that of their society, required radical change. As long as they refused to look into the poverty of their own hearts, Merton could see that their good intentions for the blacks would remain flirtations, and all their so-called help only apparent concessions. Without realising it, a feeling of contempt can easily creep into our denunciation of the deeds of the wicked.

We cannot remind ourselves often enough that Christ died even for the most unscrupulous politician and for all others who mislead and corrupt their fellow human beings. The Church must not seek to fulfil its prophetic function to society in a spirit of self-righteousness. In our desire to help others we must be willing to change ourselves. The Church's role as a watchman in society requires that our service be offered in a humble spirit in the knowledge that we too are under the judgement and mercy of the Gospel. Ours is never more than a very spotted form of virtue. Selwyn Dawson, a New Zealand priest, captures the ambiguity and ambivalence of our caring when he writes:

> This is where I come up against another truth about myself, and a very uncomfortable one: I just can't treat every person as Christ. So here I am in a cleft stick. If I am to take my gospel seriously, I have to see Christ in the stumbling fellow who rings my doorbell, and God help me, I just can't. What is the way out of my dilemma? I'll tell you! I have to learn to live as a failure, a defaulter — a sinner — but one who knows that he is forgiven, who knows that while the obligation still binds me, I shan't be disqualified because I can't keep it: instead I have to keep trying, keep breasting up to my obligation to see Christ in every person, and yet to live with the fact that I am forgiven — and that if I really care, he will help me next time to come a little closer to my goal.[7]

Contemplative carers are those who have allowed the Gospel to seep into their very beings so that as they watch for the coming of Christ in the poor and marginalised, they know that their self-worth is not determined by pleasing others but by God's unconditional acceptance of them. They are liberated from the bitter idealism, self-righteousness and complacency that threatens to overwhelm the lives of many social activists. Their service is 'perfect freedom'.

---

7 S. Dawson, in *The Expository Times*, Vol.86, 1974–75, p.82.

CHAPTER SEVEN

WHEN THIRST IS FINALLY QUENCHED

'THE HALF HAS NOT BEEN TOLD ME'

Monasticism makes no sense to those who have no doctrine of heaven. The life of a monk remains an enigma in a society where people live in a down-to-earth, matter-of-fact, this-worldly manner. But once it is conceded that life is lived in two overlapping stages, 'this age' and 'the age to come', it is possible to begin to see that what may appear to be wasted time and effort, when measured against a this-worldly view of life, takes on an altogether different look when measured against a bigger, broader canvas. Monasticism presses home St Paul's assertion that 'if it is for this life only that Christ has given us hope, we of all people are most to be pitied' (1 Corinthians 15:19). The apostle declares that this life is not definitive. Cut off from the next life, Christianity is the ultimate foolishness. A monk's life stands as a witness against every perception of reality that is finite. Apart from a belief in the doctrine of heaven it makes no sense whatever. More positively, monasticism's eschatological orientation (that is, its concern for the ultimate goal of history) says to the world and to the Church: 'No earthly good can be worth dying for unless there is a heavenly good that is worth living for.'

There is a tendency among some contemporary evangelists to suggest that a life of bliss is possible in the here and now, as though complete satisfaction can be ours this side of heaven. Such teaching has the effect of blunting the painful reality of what it is like to live as part of an imperfect and sometimes evil community. In the letter to the Romans the apostle Paul makes it clear that until our final redemption, when Christ will return to knit back together the torn fabric of heaven and earth, we and the whole creation, animate and inanimate, will 'groan' for what we do not have (Romans 8:23).

Uncovering Our Deep Longings

Beneath the surface of everyone's life there is an ache that will not go away. It can be ignored, disguised, submerged by a torrent of activity, but it will not go away. And that for good reason. We were designed to enjoy a better world than this. C. S. Lewis has written much on this theme. In a sermon preached in 1941 he said:

> … if we consider the unblushing promises of reward and the staggering nature of the rewards promised in the gospels, it would seem that our Lord finds our desires, not too strong, but too weak. We are half-hearted creatures, fooling about with drink and sex and ambition when infinite joy is offered us, like an ignorant child who wants to go on making mud pies in the slum because he cannot imagine what is meant by the offer of a holiday at the sea. We are far too easily pleased.[1]

1 C. S. Lewis, *The Weight of Glory and other Essays,* Grand Rapids: Eerdmans, 1965, pp.1,2.

Our deep longings are part of our humanness and therefore there is no need to be ashamed of them. An aching soul is evidence not of neurosis or spiritual immaturity but of realism. Our only hope for relief is the advent of Christ and the new and perfect world that awaits us in the good plan of God. Even Chrysostom, the golden-tongued preacher of Antioch, finds that language cannot cope with the surpassing grandeur of Christ's final return. Speaking of that moment, he says:

> Then is the whole heaven thrown open, and the gates of those concaves unfold themselves, and the only-begotten Son of God descends, not with twenty, not with a hundred men for his body guard, but with thousands and ten thousands of angels and archangels, cherubim and seraphim, and other powers, and with fear and trembling shall every thing be filled, while the earth is being torn apart, and all who ever lived, from Adam's birth up to that day, rise from the earth and are caught up: at that time, he himself will then appear with such glory, that the moon and the sun, and all light, will be cast into the shade, being out-shone by the radiance. What language can capture for us that blessedness, brightness, glory?... But still our sights are fixed in this present world, and we take no notice of the devil's cunning, who by little things bereaves us of those great things, and gives us clay that he may snatch from us gold, or rather he may snatch heaven from us, and shows us a shadow in exchange for the reality ...[2]

To modern ears such talk of heaven can sound like pie-in-the-sky kind of comfort. To a generation that looks for relief now, it is hopelessly non-immediate. To be told that we have to wait until we get to heaven to find the answers to life's enigmas seems unbearable. And yet, the Scriptures refer frequently to the fact that the deep longings of the human heart are universal. The

---

2 NPNF Vol.11, Hom.14 in Rom, p.450.

ancient writer of Ecclesiastes was aware of the dignity of humankind when he said that God had set eternity in the human mind (Ecclesiastes 3:11). This author knew that God is the goal we were made for; the Eternal towards whom the 'eternity in the human mind' was meant to gravitate. Such eternal yearning forms the basis of all prayer. The human heart is smitten with an intractable desire for that which is infinite and everlasting.

Sometimes the Biblical literature describes this human longing in terms of thirst. It is not a surprising image given the shortage of water in Palestine for a large part of each year. The climate is suitable for a camel. It is an animal with its own built-in water conservation equipment. For the wild deer it is very different. The deer longs for the running water of the Palestinian creeks and waddies that only flow for a short period each year. It strains forward after the very smell or sound of running water:

> As a deer longs for flowing streams,
> so my soul longs for you, O God.
> My soul thirsts for God,
> for the living God. (Psalm 42:1,2)

At other times the longing for God is described in the Bible as a deep desire.

> Whom have I in heaven but you?
> And there is nothing on earth that I desire other than you.
> My flesh and my heart may fail, but God is the strength
> of my heart and my portion forever. (Psalm 73:25,26)

God's presence was thought to be located in the temple, for the temple was by definition the divine dwelling place. The image is very simple. If you want to see a man, you go to his house. If you want to see God, you go to God's house. But this material location of God's presence did not prevent it being a deep spiritual reality. Both the longing and the desire of which the Scriptures speak are attitudes with which we can identify.

The psalmist's imagery is expressive of the deep personal attraction for God of which Professor P. Hanson has written so compellingly:

> I want to believe in God and I do believe in God because I cannot resist the attraction which such belief holds for me. Over a long period, about 35 years, I have found that belief in God as he is understood in the Christian religion attracts me so deeply that I cannot stop believing unless I turn against the deepest inclination of my heart.[3]

Professor Hanson makes the further point that:

> ... the fact that a person wants to believe something is no proof of the truth of that belief, but it is no disproof either. I want to believe that my wife loves me. This is no disproof of the proposition which I want to believe. Further there is nothing discreditable in wanting to believe such a comfortable doctrine, nor in deriving pleasure in believing it. Because a belief gives somebody pleasure and comfort it does not follow that the belief must be untrue ... Psychology has made people suspicious of beliefs which are hopeful or comforting... Too many people today in considering the subject of God submit to what might be called psychological intimidation. They give in easily when other people explain to them why they believe what they believe'.[4]

Grace Jantzen has argued that an important way to encourage spiritual growth is to 'bear witness to the sheer beauty of God, the wonder of divine attractiveness. The greatest blasphemy is to make God dull.'[5]

Such longing for God is the work of the Holy Spirit.

---

3 P. Hanson, *The Attractiveness of God*, SPCK, 1973, p.1.

4 Ibid., p.2.

5 G. Jantzen, *Theology*, March 1989.

It is the Spirit who entices us, luring us to pay attention to God. It is the Spirit who creates the thirst and desire for God. Both these themes have exercised a dominant influence on monastic spirituality, especially in the West. Based on these underlying realities the monastic writers developed an anthropology (the study of humankind) that was pivotal to their life of prayer. Thirst or desire for God arises from the fact that human beings have been 'made in the image of God' (Genesis 1:26,27). It is this that gives humanity a compatibility or affinity with God. As human beings move towards God in prayer and meditation, they become more profoundly human. As they turn away from God, they deny their true identity. They become sub-human. Prayer as an expression of desire for God is not therefore a distortion of human nature. It is a natural part of being fully human.

St Augustine (354–430) is the great poet and theologian of this everlasting longing of the human heart. Human creatures are looking, longing, waiting for God, and nothing that is not God will satisfy the God-need. Augustine knew this from his own experience. In his *Confessions* he writes:

> Late have I loved You, O beauty so ancient and so
> new, late have I loved You. For see, You were within
> and I was without, and I sought you out there.
> Unlovely, I rushed heedlessly among the lovely things
> you made. You were with me, but I was not with
> You. These things kept me far from You: even though
> they were not at all unless they were in You.

Those who, like Augustine, experience the pain of thirst, are better equipped to recognise the deceitful allure of lesser pleasures. But though the theme of desire is most prominent in the Western tradition it is not absent from the East. Chrysostom also accepted that our hearts are already devoured by a desire to be with God and that all we need to do is to penetrate to our hearts.

He wrote: 'Find the key of your heart and you will see that it opens for you the gates of the kingdom.'

The entire basis for prayer, in Chrysostom as in the New Testament, is a longing for the coming of the kingdom of God. The much loved Collect for Purity, said as a prayer of preparation for the Eucharist in Anglican liturgies, acknowledges the presence of desires in the human heart and asks that the Holy Spirit may both remove the sooty touch of sin which distorts those desires and refashion them so that they point again in a Godward direction:

> Almighty God,
> to whom all hearts are open,
> all desires known,
> and from whom no secrets are hidden:
> cleanse the thoughts of our hearts
> by the inspiration of your Holy Spirit,
> that we may perfectly love you,
> and worthily magnify your holy name,
> through Christ our Lord. Amen.

SORROW, SEX, PAIN AND PATIENCE

Sometimes we look for a kind of change God hasn't promised. We try to suppress the necessary pain of living in this world. I recall my own personal confusion when my mother was killed in a car accident on the outskirts of Darwin. It was frightening to feel, as I felt then, that life was out of control. In retrospect I see how important it was to allow myself to feel the confusion. It was an essential part of the grieving process which I as a Christian felt tempted to suppress. The nagging questions might have gone away if I had reminded myself that 'all things work together for the good of those who love God …' (Romans 8:28). The problem is that when truth is offered for the purpose of shutting down hard questions, that truth becomes a cliché. Instead, I allowed the many questions that arose in my pain to burst open my tidy theological mind to confusion. This was a confusion I needed to enter rather than a state of numbness. Sugar-coating with Biblical texts is not helpful in the long term. Radical self-honesty is much more helpful.

This is where the help of a spiritual director or 'soul-friend' can be so valuable. If, however, we are to derive help from a such a person we must be prepared, as Michael Casey has said, 'to go beyond comfortable limits, to act contrary to our sense of shame, to ignore our own blushes'. Churches are not conspicuous for encouraging this kind of radical self-honesty. This is especially the case in regard to the struggle with sexuality.

I only can write from the experience of a half-century-old male. Explicit sexuality makes a relatively late appearance in our consciousness. Ideally it would be much easier if there could be an instant integration of sexuality into our character. The physical aspects of puberty for the young male can be an embarrassing nuisance. The truth is, however, such an ideal is rarely realised without considerable struggle over a longer period of time than many of us would care to admit. Middle age does not seem to be automatically refining my appetites. Unholy desires can still burn within me.

Perfect harmony between the sexual side of our characters and our religious and moral values is not instantaneous. Pain, mistakes and confusion are par for the course. Most of us, at puberty or later on, tend to one extreme or another. Either we try to carry on as normal, denying our sexuality and longing for pre-puberty 'innocence' or we allow it to control us.

The single life, for instance, is sometimes lived as a solitary existence devoid of relationships and one where all awareness of sexuality is rejected or, at the most, kept quiet as a guilty secret. When that is true, either by design or default, life is severely impoverished and growth inevitably stunted. As one of the Tarrawarra monks has said: 'Sex is a big part of human life and the urge certainly does not go away when you enter a monastery.'

A homosexual Christian writes of how he finds, in the midst of his burning torment, some comfort from the hope of the flawless perfection that awaits him in heaven. He says:

> The fact that the Spirit already dwells in me, so that
> in spite of frequent failure I truly do delight in the
> law of God after the inward man, is the guarantee
> that one day the renewal of the body will follow. And
> the sooner the better, say I: roll on eternity![6]

Our bodies, whose faults and infirmities cause us so much trouble in this world, will be raised and recreated in perfection for the world to come. When we sense our mediocrity and reluctance to change, we can take consolation in the fact that the outstanding figures of Church history such as St Augustine, often defaulted by praying: 'Yes, but not yet!' In this life, all of us are fragmented, 'parts outside parts'. In heaven, we will enjoy the total and simultaneous possession of complete and abundant life. Like Augustine, even as we pray 'tomorrow and tomorrow', a storm steadily begins to build within us. Sooner or later our own mediocrity will sicken us and we will cry out: 'Why not now?'

Although Augustine's conversion was sudden it took a lifetime to work out. Monastic spirituality places a great deal of emphasis on the fact that Christian maturity is a gradual process. Benedict wrote his 'little Rule for beginners' (RB 73). Nothing was to be required that was 'harsh or burdensome'. For Benedict, no matter how

---

6 A. Davidson, *The Returns of Love*, IVP, 1970, p.49.

intense a monk's efforts or how long a person has been a monk, they are never more than beginners in the spiritual life.

The novice knows that when he enters the monastery he is in for a long haul. He will be chiselling away at the darkness within until the day he dies. 'Believe me,' said one of the early desert Fathers, Abba Theodore, 'I have been seventy years in this habit and I have never been able to find even a single day of rest.' In his weary struggle with his own inner dividedness the monk can easily become depressed to the point of desperation. It is essential therefore that patience be suffused with a buoyancy that makes it a positive force for good. Cardinal Basil Hume, writing out of first-hand experience says:

> It takes some years of experience in monastic life to
> recognise that consciousness of failure and frailty
> must not lead to despondency, but rather to complete
> trust and confidence in God's help. We have to move
> from preoccupation with our own perfection to an
> intense interest in the perfection of God.[7]

And what is true for the monk is true for every baptised Christian. There are some who find it hard not to expect perfection of themselves and because of that they expect it of others as well. But baptism which is a once-in-a-lifetime experience takes a whole life to complete. For that reason we must be patient with one another's growth.

The monastic stress on patience can serve as a warning against all quack practitioners of the soul who promise instant holiness by a given formula or experience. We are a society of instant coffee, microwave ovens and same-day service. We want things and we want them now. Some Christians place an unhealthy

---

7 B. Hume, *In Praise of Benedict*, Hodder and Stoughton, 1981, p.20.

emphasis on a once-for-all experience that settles past, present, and future. But every Christian is a pilgrim. Our spiritual autobiography is still in the making. Premature attempts to finish the 'story' either at conversion, baptism or a 'second blessing,' are to be resisted.

A contemplative, as Bernard of Clairvaux says, is not merely one for whom to live is Christ, but one for whom this has been the case for a long time. In Australian terms, the Christian life is like a walk across the vast Nullarbor Plain. Every step is progress but there is always such a long way to go! The recognition of God's undeserved love can free us from needing to be better than we are and free us to face what we are really like without giving up.

HEAVEN ANTICIPATED

The necessity of patience in the face of present heart-breaks and struggles may serve only to produce an unattractive, unexciting and lifeless practice of disciplined religion. Such an attitude is miles removed from the 'joy unspeakable' referred to in the New Testament (1 Peter 1:8). Striving for heavenly perfection can be a boring way of spending one's time on earth! It is only when the longing for heaven is seen as a longing for closer communion with Christ that it can begin to impact on the quality of our lives now. Our problem is not that we are too passionate about bad things but that we are not passionate enough about the things that really matter. Only an all-consuming love can turn a lifeless religion into joyful discipleship. Then, what we are required to sacrifice — the 'crosses and losses' — will pale into insignificance compared to what we have gained. For the apostle Paul, no cost seemed too great for the privilege of intimacy with Christ:

> Yet whatever gains I had, these I have come to regard
> as loss because of Christ. More than that, I regard
> everything as loss because of the surpassing value of
> knowing Christ Jesus my Lord. For his sake I have
> suffered the loss of all things, and I regard them as
> rubbish, in order that I may gain Christ and be found
> in him ... (Philippians 3:7–9)

Pain is an inevitable part of living in a fallen world.
It is not, however, until we acknowledge confusion and
heartache in our circumstances and relationships that
we will pursue Christ with the passion of deep thirst.

The fact that we cannot have heaven on earth does
not mean that we are denied a foretaste of what is in
store for us. We must not allow ourselves to go to the
other extreme in adopting a 'vale of tears' theology.
Through the Holy Spirit, we can indeed anticipate something of our future bliss. The Spirit is the 'pledge' or
'guarantee' that the best is yet to be, a sample in
advance of the life of heaven (2 Corinthians 1:22, 5:5
and Ephesians 1:14). As the 'Lord and giver of life', the
Spirit is pre-eminently the gift of aliveness to God's people.
It is through the ministry of the Spirit that we come alive
towards other people, we come alive to the glory and
tragedy of this world and we come alive towards the
reality of ourselves. More than that, we come alive to the
vast, embracing joy of God. These are all hints of a more
permanent aliveness which follows the Christian's death.
It is the Spirit that prompts the Christian to think of life
with all its twists and turns as, 'all this! — and heaven
too'. Through the Spirit's gift of aliveness we can begin
to enjoy in part the banquet table God will one day
spread before us.

TOMORROW AND TOMORROW AND TOMORROW

There are many who take the view that those who live in monasteries are escaping from the uncomfortable grimness of reality. Alvin Toffler has spoken of those who react to the speed of change with 'the psychological lust for the simpler, less turbulent past'. He warns that it is a foolish mistake to drive headlong into the future 'with our eyes fixed on our rear-view mirrors'. There are no doubt some who perceive monasticism in this way. Monks dressed in medieval habits and chanting plainsong are regarded as people who are phoney or antique, running away from a world that is changing at blinding speed. Clearly the world has changed so vastly that it would be foolish to try to live in the monastic world of the sixth century, even if it were possible. But it is not and such a view completely fails to take into account the future-looking, eschatological perspective which I have argued has always been a dominant strand of monastic mentality. Monks have always taken the future with full seriousness. Society at large, and the Church in particular, cannot fail to do less. The continuing witness of this future strand of Gospel truth is more than ever necessary as we come to the threshold of a new millennium.

When Christian eschatology falls into disfavour it is inevitably replaced by the secular eschatologies of Nazism, Fascism and optimistic humanism. Human beings find it difficult to live without a concept of something ultimate which still lies in the future. Relativism is convenient, and yet our being cries out for something more.

The only way humanity can live responsibly in a rapidly changing world is by learning to anticipate and respond to the future. On the world scene, great strides have been made in recent years in reducing the likelihood of nuclear disaster. But the secret of nuclear power cannot be disinvented. If nuclear disaster through military action seems a remote possibility at present there is always the risk of industrial accident. The problem that faces the modern world is not simply moral, political or ecological. It is theological: how to help humankind live with hope in the face of the fear of global disaster. Such a hope will be more than optimism because it will take its cue on how to face the future from Christ rather than the bomb.

Nor can the monastic vision of a better future be made to square with the Western dream of a better life. Modern educationalists appear more intent on helping young people to fit into middle-class professions and life-styles than involving them in a vision that can turn the world upside down. Monasticism stands out from the pervading materialistic and hedonistic dreams of modern educationalists as a counter-cultural movement. In its true form it is not to be thought of as some kind of neo-primitivism, interested only in long flowing robes and physically remote places. Its concern is not with the cosmetic matters of where we live and what we wear but with what fills our minds. The physical distance of the monastery from towns and cities is intended to be a pointer to the 'behavioural distance' which all Christians, whatever their calling, are to show in relation to worldly thinking and materialistic living. The fundamental difference shows up at the deeper level of the mind and heart, for 'where your treasure is, there will your heart be also'.

This does not mean that monasticism turns away from the problems of the world to contemplate a better future in the clouds. As we have seen, thinkers like John Chrysostom, have been used to deflect monasticism from such outmoded superstition. Chrysostom had imparted a vision of a God who participates fully in both the pain and the hope that fills our world. He believed that the coming of the Lord is not restricted to the final curtain descent at the end of history. The 'age to come' has already intruded into, and is now being established, in 'this age' through the ministry of Word, Sacrament and service to the needy. The future of God is not to be understood as some escapist notion that allows us to make peace with unrighteousness on earth. Rather, it is the divine tug that motivates the reform of the present state of things.

More than ever, we need to recover this vision of the One who keeps on coming in accordance with his covenanted promise to be with us always, in Word, Sacrament and the persons of our needy sisters and brothers. Whenever he is tempted to become self-absorbed and depressed about the future, Bishop Richard Holloway, the Primus of the Church of Scotland, recalls a few lines of poetry, written by a member of an enclosed order, which he once saw on a retreat house noticeboard:

Look back, remember, and have confidence;
The future, like the past, has God in it;
His cupped hands bear the whole of time, and you;
The future holds nothing which can elude
His covenanted care and mastery.

The One who in 'covenanted care and mastery' keeps on coming in the present is the One who will finally come again to swallow up all the difficulties of life. Nor do we have to live with the nagging fear that something terrible might happen tomorrow. In every sense, our future is with God.

Jesus: Our Story

FRANK ANDERSEN MSC

Jesus: Our Story is the fruit of a lifetime's prayer and pondering of the Gospels. Through creative presentation of key Gospel stories, suggestions for imaginative prayer and questions suitable for personal or group reflection, Frank Andersen MSC leads readers into an encounter with Jesus that can change lives.

Fr Andersen writes from his conviction that in the person of Jesus we discover the meaning of our own humanity – that the story of *Jesus* is *Our Story*. In meeting Jesus, we see the human face of God, and discover the call and the power 'to be on earth the heart of God'.

'This is a book to be read, pondered and reflected upon, then discussed. It challenges our understanding of ourselves and of Jesus.'
PENELOPE MADDICK
National Catholic Education Commission

Frank Andersen, a Missionary of the Sacred Heart priest, is best known as a composer of contemporary hymns, the collections of which are *Eagle's Wings*, *Everything I Possess*, *Rising Moon* and *Kindly Light*. Fr Andersen has wide experience as a retreat director and liturgist, and is currently part of a team engaged in adult faith formation in parishes and schools.

CollinsDove
An imprint of HarperCollins*Publishers*

$14.95
ISBN 1863713816

The HarperCollins Study Bible

WAYNE A. MEEKS (general editor)

How many of us *really* understand the Bible?

A study bible for the 21st Century, *The HarperCollins Study Bible* contains a library of information in one convenient, authoritative volume. It contains the full text of the New Revised Standard Version – the newest and most inclusive translation – as well as detailed annotations from sixty-one leading experts. Complete with findings from recent archaeological research, the entire Apocryphal/Deuterocanonical books, colour maps, and informative tables, *The HarperCollins Study Bible* is the definitive Bible resource.

'With its introduction to each book and its explanatory footnotes below the text, the Study Bible will help many people to a richer understanding of the Bible. With 2355 pages of text plus 18 colour maps and a hardcover binding for $49.95, it is extraordinary value for money.'

REVEREND GEOFFREY ROBINSON
Auxiliary Archbishop of Sydney

CollinsDove
An imprint of HarperCollins*Publishers*

$49.95
ISBN 60655801

Joshua: A parable for today

When Joshua moves to a small cabin on the edge of town, the local people are at first mystified, then confused by his presence. What sort of person is Joshua? How can the townspeople explain a few rumours about him? Some people report seeing him carry a huge oak log on his shoulders. Effortlessly. And others talk about the child in a poor part of town who was dreadfully ill. After Joshua's visit, she recovered immediately.

Yet the woodcarver Joshua disturbs some of his neighbours. While he quietly and lovingly urges all around him to break down the walls that separate them, there are others who are frightened of him. Finally, some church leaders confront him...

Here is a profoundly moving, deeply inspiring book that no reader will ever forget. Already, *Joshua* has been called 'life-changing', 'engrossing', 'inspiring', 'entertaining'. Based on a scrupulously accurate reading of scripture, *Joshua* has universal appeal and is a true exercise in spirituality. Once you've read it, you'll want everyone you love to read it, too.

CollinsDove
An imprint of HarperCollins*Publishers*

$14.95
ISBN 1 86371 100 7